AMPLIFY YOUR BUSINESS

VOLUME 1

THE *Rockstar* PROFESSIONAL'S GUIDE TO MARKETING SUCCESS

The Action Marketing Platform (AMP) Series by

ROCK MY IMAGE

ISBN-10: 0-9972695-0-2
ISBN-13: 978-0-9972695-0-5
LCCN: 2016940232

Editorial assistance provided by Kimberly Smith Ashley and KM Smith Writes. www.KMSmithWrites.com. Writing and editing for industry authorities.

RockMyImage.com

Printed in the United States of America
Second Edition February, 2017

VISIT ROCKMYIMAGE.COM/AMPLIFY TO ACCESS THESE FREE RESOURCES:

- Vision & Mission Guide
- Personal Branding Checklist
- MAP (Marketing Action Plan) Printable
- SWOT Analysis Printable

PLUS THESE BONUSES

- An electronic copy of *Amplify Your Business: The Rockstar Professional's Guide to Marketing Success*
- Audio book files for listening on-the-go

A $347 VALUE IS ALL YOURS FOR FREE!

Visit **www.rockmyimage.com/amplify** to claim your free tools & resources

SOCIAL

facebook.com/rockmyimage

@rockmyimagejax

instagram.com/rockmyimage

linkedin.com/company/rock-my-image

To all the current and
future Rockstar Professionals

THINK BOLD. AIM HIGH. ROCK ON.

Joanie,
Thanks for being an inspiration
and a Rockstar Professional!
ROCK ON!
Kenny

CONTENTS

Introduction: Moving Off Zero 1

But First, a Reality Check 3

Amplify and Succeed!
Meet the Rockstar Professional (RP) 4

Enter Rock My Image 6

RMI's Unique Selling Proposition 10

The Action Marketing Platform (AMP)™ Series 11

Leaving Level Zero 17

Level 1: Getting in Tune—Clear Objective, Bold Vision, Inspired Mission, and Reasoned Motivation 19

Level 1 Gains: The 4 Keys for Getting in Tune 19

Level 1 Key Terms 20

Level 1 Self-Assessment 20

Defining Your Clear Objective 21

Setting Your Bold Vision 24

Establishing Your Inspired Mission 26

Understanding Your Reasoned Motivation 30

Level 1 Amplifiers and Tweaks 40

Level 1 Dialers and Drainers 40

Level 2: Sharpening Your Awareness—
You Are Your Story 43

Level 2 Gains: The 5 Chords of Branding Yourself 44

Level 2 Key Terms 44

Level 2 Self-Assessment 45

Understanding Your Core Competencies 45

Crafting Your Story 53

Identifying Your Unique Selling Proposition 55

Connecting with Your Audience 63

Upping Your Game 68

Level 2 Amplifiers and Tweaks 81

Level 2 Dialers and Drainers 82

Level 3: Planning to Rock—Smart Marketing Planning, Strategic Marketing Decisions 85

Level 3 Gains: The 4 Cs of Strategic Marketing 86

Level 3 Key Terms 86

Level 3 Self-Assessment 87

Committing to a Marketing Budget 87

Creating a 1-Page Marketing Action Plan 91

Conserving Your Time and Money 104

Choosing Tactics Strategically 109

Level 3 Amplifiers and Tweaks 114

Level 3 Dialers and Drainers 115

Summation: Level 1-3 Gains and Moving Forward 117

Sound Bites: A Preview of Levels 4-7—

Boost Your Business: The Rockstar Professional's Guide to Marketing Success Volume 2 119

Liner Notes 123

INTRODUCTION
MOVING OFF ZERO

Like a modern-day music festival, often in business the "stage" is packed with performers, both bands and solo acts. Competition for audience time is fierce. Potential for exposure is great. Rewards in terms of sales and publicity are on all the performers' minds. As with any music fest—for example, Woodstock (if you're of that generation) or Lollapalooza and Coachella (for today's fest-goers)—the stakes are high and the payoffs tremendous, but you have to be invited and, once on stage, you have to do more than just deliver; you have to nail it. You have to rock the house, if you will. The AMP series is for those businesses and professionals with the desire to be "rock stars" in their industries and willing to put forth the time and effort it takes to make it to the metaphorical stage and to bring it full force once arrived.

When considering what it takes to be a Rockstar Professional in today's business climate, a Greek proverb comes to mind: "From a broken violin do not expect fine music." Perhaps you're reading Volume 1 of the AMP series because you feel as if your "violin" is broken. Perhaps not. You may be strumming along and getting results with your marketing efforts but believe more information is always a good idea. Whatever the case and however you perceive yourself in the business market today, we invite you to start this action marketing journey with us at what we call Level Zero, where we'll establish the way in which we envision becoming a Rockstar Professional (RP): by achieving gains on ten distinct levels and reaching Level 11, the RP. At this level, we'll also introduce you to Rock My Image, our bold vision and inspired mission, and the creative minds behind our marketing stage.

Don't worry, though; starting at Level Zero isn't about throwing away or discounting the hard work you may have put into your marketing plan. It's about recognizing that what you may already have in place may or may not be working for you and that there may be room for improvement. Also, it's about accepting that now is the perfect time for examining where you are on the levels to becoming the marketing rock star of your own business or industry and achieving the marketing results you desire. If you haven't put into place certain necessary elements, achieving gains on the ten levels to becoming an RP, then it's certainly time to examine your current standing and *move off Level Zero.*

BUT FIRST, A REALITY CHECK

Before introducing the 11 Levels, let's agree on a basic truth: Business can be brutal. Just as in rock 'n' roll, in business it's a long way to the top. Becoming an overnight success, or even creating a one-hit wonder, is unlikely to improbable at best. Sure, a few lucky businesses miraculously achieve success by being in the right place with the right idea at the right time. The overwhelming majority of businesses, however, achieve success the old-fashioned way: one mouse click, one sale, one project at a time—getting up every day and committing to do the work . . . for years.

Here's the reality check: Most businesses fail, and yours may too. According to *Bloomberg* magazine,[1] 80 percent of businesses fail in the first 18 months. Businesses fail for many reasons, but one underlying cause is universal: lack of knowledge.

In most cases, it is lack of knowledge in a key part of the business—such as marketing, finances, operations, logistics, or staffing—that crashes a business. What we as Rockstar Professionals ourselves witness is that business owners have "passion" for their businesses but lack the knowledge needed to make the business sustainable, especially in terms of strategic marketing. In most cases, they have not built a solid marketing platform. If you can use your passion to fuel you, combine it with the knowledge needed to make the right marketing decisions, and *do* the work, you *can* be one of the few success stories.

AMPLIFY AND SUCCEED! MEET THE ROCKSTAR PROFESSIONAL (RP)

Maybe 80 percent of businesses fail in the first 18 months, but you can be part of that 20 percent who succeed. Furthermore, with the AMP series and its concepts, not only can you survive the first 18 months, but also you can *Amplify Your Business* (AMP Volume 1), *Boost Your Business* (AMP Volume 2), and *Rock Your Business* (AMP Volume 3) all the way to the top.

At Rock My Image, we believe the best chance business professionals and company owners have to reach a high level of success is to achieve specific marketing gains through taking strategic action. In doing so, such a person becomes a Rockstar Professional (RP). Consider some characteristics of RPs:

- Crystal clear about their objective
- Fearless in setting their bold vision
- Fueled by their inspired mission
- Driven by their reasoned motivation
- Willing to brand their story for marketing success
- Make SMART plans and goals
- Add to their core knowledge and skill base routinely
- Position themselves as industry authorities
- Can turn a customer into an avid fan
- Maximize their marketing investments
- Leverage the right tools and systems for marketing success

- Reflect, refine, and repeat marketing efforts
- Evolve with the market

In today's competitive market, it's not enough to make a haphazard marketing effort and then sit back and wait for customers to bang down your door. We've found, though, that they'll clamor for your products and services if you set the stage for marketing success, follow through with a strategic marketing action plan, and consistently fine-tune your efforts. If you're willing to take these actions, you will become an RP.

IS THIS BOOK FOR YOU?

We know this book and the AMP series may not be for every professional or business owner. Not everyone wants to think this deeply about marketing. Fewer still are willing to invest the time and energy it takes to amplify their businesses. Like the reality that 80 percent of businesses fail in the first 18 months, it's a reality that reaching Rockstar Professional level is unique and rare. You may be, however, of that distinctive class. To begin this journey, you'll need to ask yourself two questions:

1. Do you want to rock your business?
2. Are you willing to do the work it takes?

If you answered yes to both those questions, then this book *is* for you.

ENTER ROCK MY IMAGE

We think it's no stretch to proclaim that Rock My Image is the *authority in authority marketing*. We are an authority marketing agency that helps business owners create an image of influence, build online sales funnels, and capitalize on their expertise. To us, being a "Rockstar" Professional means being exceptional at what you do, having a story to tell, and helping others through your expertise.

Combined, the Rock My Image partners, Kenny Harper, Jen DeVore Richter, and Manny Torres have over fifty years of marketing experience. We've worked with large brands such as Kennedy Space Center and Porsche North America, and we've spent the last decade or so proving our marketing expertise to hundreds of local businesses and professional practices.

We're leaders in our industry and professional speakers, as well. Frequently, we're asked to guest teach at the university level, and we present to professional business groups and associations regularly. We are family centered, goal oriented, and die-hard fans of the entrepreneurial spirit.

RMI'S BOLD VISION AND INSPIRED MISSION

What we've come to understand and ask our clients to embrace is that to be a Rockstar Professional and achieve amazing marketing success you need a ***bold vision*** and ***inspired mission***. A bold vision and inspired mission, set the stage for marketing success, and not just expected success but success that rockets businesses into the most fantastic heights.

One should not overlook or gloss over these important elements. Too many businesses and professionals rush these crucial marketing elements in order to get out there and start selling customers or servicing clients. Often, they discover that without a bold vision and inspired mission their marketing efforts are scattershot and ineffective. We'll explore more about setting a bold vision and establishing an inspired mission in Level 1. For now, we'd love to share ours.

THE AMP™ BOLD VISION

Ignite your message to amplify business growth and achieve excellence.

THE AMP™ INSPIRED MISSION

Rock My Image is an authority marketing agency that provides business owners with marketing solutions that are innovative, engaging, and worthy of "Rockstar" status. We use our creative insight and proven marketing approach to build brands, craft tools, and implement plans that earn attention and garner results.

THE CREATIVE MINDS BEHIND ROCK MY IMAGE

Our bold vision and inspired mission drive us every day, *and yours will too*, if you take the time to think through both carefully and then implement each deliberately and in a focused way. Your future success is in your hands. That may be a daunting or frightening prospect to some, but you're that rare caliber of professional that relishes such freedom to shape your destiny, a key quality to becoming a Rockstar Professional. So are we!

Our cofounders' bios express our entrepreneurial spirit and our passion for creativity.

KENNY HARPER |

Cofounder, Rock My Image

Kenny Harper is a marketing industry standout and leader, inspired business owner, and professional speaker on a mission to encourage others to bring their passions to life. Kenny gleans from his experience as a former advertising agency digital developer, technical certifications, and systems expertise to produce digital marketing strategies that are creative, effective, and scalable. As a business owner for over eleven years, Kenny has successfully led the digital development of two agencies and now directs the technical teams and systems development efforts of Rock My Image.

Kenny is happily married to his wife Kathy and is a proud father of their two boys, Kenny and Michael. He is honored to instill in them his passions for music, creativity, personal growth, and living a fulfilled life. **www.kennyharper.rocks**

JEN DeVORE RICHTER

Cofounder, Rock My Image

Jen DeVore Richter is a marketing expert, seasoned business owner and influencer. She is frequently asked to speak professionally to women's business groups. After an achievement-filled career as a corporate marketing executive, she made the transition into entrepreneurship in 2003. Jen ran first her own award-winning photography studio and then a marketing consulting firm for nine years. In 2012, Jen cofounded Rock My Image, where she spearheads strategic planning for all agency accounts.

Jen is an active member of her church and regular participant in their community volunteer initiatives. In her spare time, she takes acting workshops and attends local community theatre events. She enjoys traveling with her husband Will, is a "bonus mom" to his two teenage children, and is an avid painter and home cook. **www.jendevore.rocks**

MANNY TORRES

Cofounder, Rock My Image

Manny Torres is a brand development expert, experienced business owner, and connector among Jacksonville's executive circles. Manny is the creative director for Rock My Image, leading a team of graphic designers and creatives, and a Certified Marketing Automation Specialist. Marketing automation is a category of technology that allows companies to streamline, automate, and measure marketing tasks and workflows so that they can increase operational efficiency and grow revenue faster.

As a board member and leader in multiple professional organizations, Manny aims to move the business community forward as a whole while contributing his unique insights on creative direction and marketing automation. At the printing of this book, he serves as president of a local Business Networkers International (BNI) chapter and on the board of directors for The Hispanic Institute for Life & Leadership (H.I.L.L.) of Northeast Florida.

Manny is happily married to his wife Mary Beth and the father to two young sons. In his spare time, he leads a men's water polo club team and hunts for the next great craft beer. **www.mannytorres.rocks**

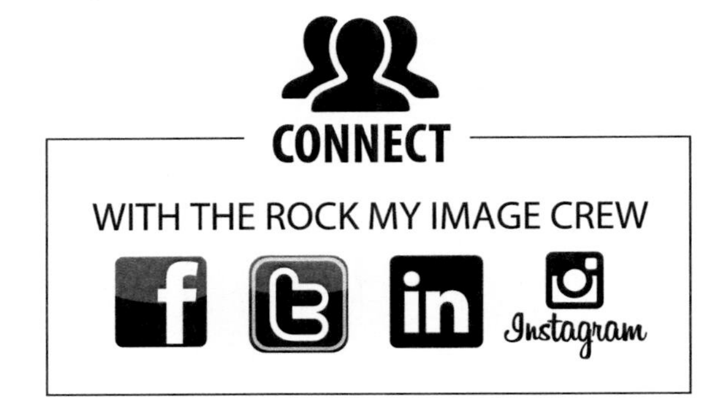

RMI'S UNIQUE SELLING PROPOSITION

Part of what we do at Rock My Image is help our clients define and communicate their unique selling proposition (USP). Our USP stems organically from our bold vision and inspired mission, and it's best represented in terms of what we do for our clients. To position you as a Rockstar Professional, we would help you:

1. Capture your bold vision—positioning you as an *authority* in your market.
2. Craft your story—creating consistent *branding* that grows a loyal fan base.
3. Connect with your audience—nurturing audience connection through dynamic *actionable marketing*.

Our USP sets us apart from run-of-the-mill marketing agencies. We help business owners create an image of influence, build online sales funnels, and capitalize on their expertise. You're already an authority in your market. We help you communicate that message in a consistently branded way through creating content that turns customers into ardent fans.

THE ACTION MARKETING PLATFORM (AMP)™ SERIES

The Action Marketing Platform (AMP)™ series provides entrepreneurs, business owners, and marketing professionals three straightforward, structured guides to improving their marketing efforts and results. The AMP volumes are not so-called how-to instructional books. Neither is the volumes meant to cover nitty-gritty technical details of individual businesses or complicated marketing concepts. The AMP series gives it to you straight, in an uncomplicated format. This approach mirrors the same real-world approach we use every day in our own successful agency and with our clients. In short, we've written the AMP series for everyone who's ever wanted to "pick our brains."

As stated earlier, the intended result of the series is to achieve gains on the ten AMP levels, ultimately reaching Level 11, Rockstar Professional. The objective of Volume 1, *Amplify Your Business*, is for the reader to move through the first 3 levels and achieve the following gains.

Amplify Your Business Gains

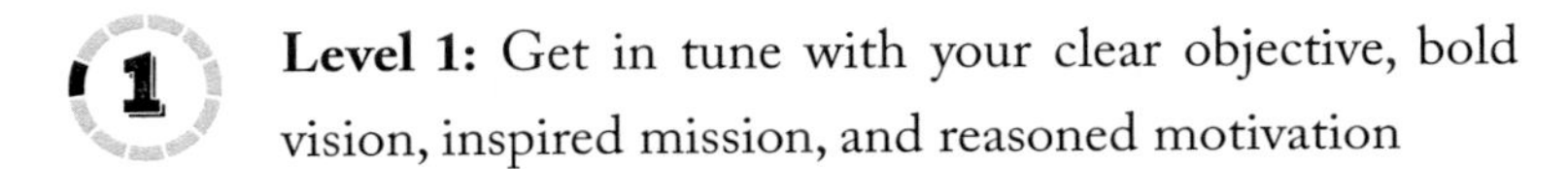

Level 1: Get in tune with your clear objective, bold vision, inspired mission, and reasoned motivation

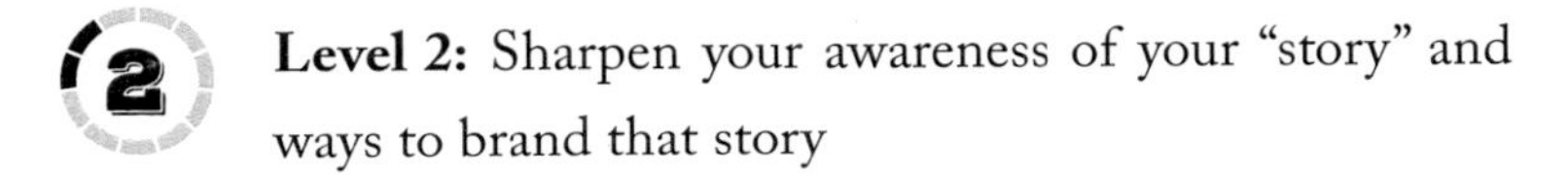

Level 2: Sharpen your awareness of your "story" and ways to brand that story

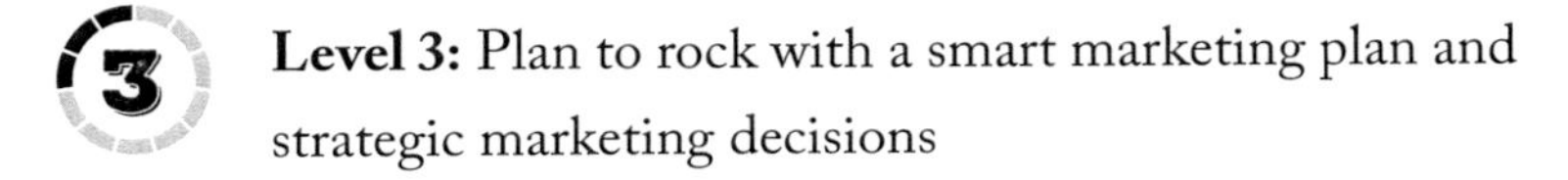

Level 3: Plan to rock with a smart marketing plan and strategic marketing decisions

Gains will be achieved at each level by self and business assessments, knowledge gains, and action items that we call Amplifiers. Completing each amplifier helps you move through the level and to the next level. Our special Dialers and Drainers section at each level gives you ways to increase your passion and practice energy-producing behaviors while avoiding energy-draining thoughts and behaviors. Along the way, we'll provide what we call Tweaks, tips and strategies to avoid leveling off and staying on the insufferable marketing "energy plateau" too long. We've designed the AMP series to create positive marketing energy and business growth. It's about movement from one level to the next.

Let's be clear: No business or professional jumps from zero straight to Level 11. Each level will provide important knowledge about that aspect of building a successful business and guide you through an amplifier that will help you achieve measurable gains in that aspect. You may be tempted to skip levels or discount this volume and rush to volumes two or three. We suggest that you resist that urge and take each level one at a time. In this way, you'll be adding to your knowledge base and strengthening any existing business elements in a deliberate, productive way. The AMP series is about success, but it's also about deliberate, focused action.

UNDERSTANDING KEY AMP TERMS

Key terms may be introduced at each level, including Level Zero, meant to help you understand the knowledge presented and better connect with the unifying framework, which is, as you've recognized by now, the metaphor of an amplifier. We'll build on this metaphor as we advance from level to level, always bearing in mind that no one metaphor can encompass all that is the world of a successful business. The amplifier image is just a means to sparking your imagination and building an amazing business.

LEVEL ZERO KEY TERMS

AMP™. The AMP™ (Action Marketing Platform) Series is intended for entrepreneurs, business owners and marketing professionals looking for a straightforward, structured guide to improve their marketing efforts and results. This is not a

"How To" instructional book or a book that covers nitty-gritty technical details or complicated marketing concepts. We're going to tell it to you straight and in an uncomplicated format to amplify your marketing.

Amplified marketing. Marketing that "pulls" customers in by providing expert knowledge and valuable information. The business professional is seen as an expert. This marketing differs from advertising that "pushes" an agenda on customers. By earning attention for your business through being an authority in your industry, you gain credibility and visibility.

Gift. The special way in which you share your talents and passion. Examples:

- I can explain complicated concepts to others in simple terms they can understand.
- Through art and/or design, I can inspire others to see things in a new way.
- I have the ability to educate and inspire others with my words.

Marketing energy. The style in which a business markets themselves has a unique energy to it. That energy can range from frenetic, high pressure, and "salesy" to calm, confident, and authoritative. Rockstar Professionals prefer to have the crowd come to them demanding to engage with them and, ultimately, to buy into their brand.

Passion. The current outlet you use to share your purpose. Examples:

- My medical practice serves patients.
- Speaking engagements are platforms for my message to a live audience.
- Online video tutorials spread my knowledge around the world.

Purpose. The way in which you or your business helps others. Examples:

- I help others make better food choices for their families.
- I help others find meaning in their careers.
- I help others reach their optimal level of health.

Rockstar Professional. A professional who's advanced from the ordinary and become an industry standout to separate oneself and share his or her unique purpose, passion, and gift.

THE 11 LEVELS OF THE AMP™ SERIES

You've read patiently about the intention of the AMP series and about RMI's bold vision and inspired mission that spark our imagination, creativity, and business drive. Perhaps you've begun considering your own bold vision, inspired mission, and your passion, purpose, and gifts. Now let's ramp things up by presenting the headlining act of the AMP Series: The 11 Levels.

1 **Level 1:** Getting in Tune—Clear Objective, Bold Vision, Inspired Mission, and Reasoned Motivation

2 **Level 2:** Sharpening Your Awareness—You Are Your Story

3 **Level 3:** Planning to Rock—Smart Marketing Planning, Strategic Marketing Decisions

4 **Level 4:** Moving Onto the Marketing Stage—The 3 Pillars of Marketing

5 **Level 5:** Positioning Yourself as an Authority for Maximum Results—Your Look, Culture, and Reality

6 **Level 6:** Turning Customers into "Avid Fans"—The Right Tools for the Job

7 **Level 7:** Maximizing Your Marketing Investment—Understanding Profitability

8 **Level 8:** Leveraging Your Tools and Systems—Fine-Tune Your Sales System and Take Action

9 **Level 9:** Adjusting Your Marketing for Peak Performance—Review, Refine, and Repeat

10 **Level 10:** Making Marketing Encores or Exits—Evolve or Exit

11 **Level 11:** Rocking Off the Charts—The Rockstar Professional

We've designed Levels 1 through 10 to take you through a systematic approach for amplified marketing success worthy of a professional operating at Level 11, reaching the status of "rock star" in your field.

ADDITIONAL RESOURCES

As you might imagine, our 11 Levels will offer a wealth of important and useful ideas and solutions in marketing to grow your business, in a way that differentiates you from your competitors. In addition to these 3 volumes on becoming a Rockstar Professional, we have created complementary resources to support this content material, including the following media:

- Podcasts
- Videos
- PDFs
- Downloads
- Other online assets

We'll continue to add advanced media to this series, so please check in with us regularly at RockMyImage.com.

LEAVING LEVEL ZERO

As we leave Level Zero, we invite you to join us in the AMP Series process and to challenge yourself to apply the concepts in this book to fulfill your vision of your professional self and your company. At times the journey may get rough. Remember the earlier statistic about failing businesses. Let us impress upon you that you *do not have to be one of the businesses that fail.* You can succeed. By applying the guides and committing diligently to its concepts, you can achieve all 11 levels and *Amplify Your Business*, then *Boost Your Business*, and, finally, *Rock Your Business*. You *can be* the Rockstar Professional you've always dreamed of becoming.

GETTING IN TUNE

Clear Objective, Bold Vision, Inspired Mission, and Reasoned Motivation

No musician wants to play an instrument that's out of tune. What would be the purpose? The sound would be distorted, the notes discordant, and the experience unpleasant for both the musician and his or her audience. Likewise, why would one set out in business without first getting in tune? Making gains at Level 1 is about striking what we call the 4 Keys for Getting in Tune in order to set a solid foundation for success. Once these key elements are tuned appropriately for your business and life goals, you'll find fine-tuning all other aspects of your business easier.

THE LEVEL 1 GAINS: THE 4 KEYS FOR GETTING IN TUNE

- Defining your clear objective
- Setting your bold vision

- Establishing your inspired mission
- Understanding your reasoned motivation

LEVEL 1 KEY TERMS

Clear Objective. The result you hope to obtain as you grow and run your business.

Bold Vision. A statement that declares a company's goals for the midterm or long-term future and identifies what the company wants to achieve or accomplish.

Inspired Mission. A statement that details a company's overall goal and pathways to that goal.

Reasoned Motivation. The energy that drives you and your business forward.

LEVEL 1 SELF-ASSESSMENT

Answer the following yes/no questions to gauge your current Level 1 readiness achievement:

1. I recognize that I have a unique story and that I can help others learn from my mistakes.
2. I may not have all the answers, but I have a clear vision of how I want my career to evolve.
3. It is important to me that others respect my business for its ideas, thought leadership, and contributions to others.

4. The thought of building my business energizes me.
5. My team and support system know my vision.

If you answered yes to all five questions, congratulations; you are ready to dig deeper into Level 1 and fine-tune your objective, vision, mission, and motivation. If you did not answer yes to each question, then get ready to explore thoroughly and establish these four important keys so that your business has the solid foundation it needs to succeed and so that you find personal fulfillment along the way.

DEFINING YOUR CLEAR OBJECTIVE

Whether you're a business owner, entrepreneur, or marketer, understanding the big picture is vital. What is your end goal? Focusing exclusively on money will not drive success forever. Your objective must encompass more than financial goals, as you are more than just a moneymaker, and a limited focus on money is ultimately draining.

While it's true that many people get into business aspiring to earn riches and gain power and freedom, many don't realize the amount of hard work and sacrifice it takes to build a successful business. These business professionals seem to suffer from an entrepreneurial seizure as detailed by Michael Gerber in *The E-Myth*. In his seminal work, Gerber describes a woman who has a love for making pies in the way taught to her by her grandmother. The woman decides that since she loves baking the pies that everyone raves about she should start her own business.

RMI POV

Goal setting is vital to making solid, functional marketing decisions and is the difference between success or failure.

Eventually, she realizes that the effort it takes to build a business means that she can't spend her time baking pies, which is why she started the business in the first place. She had no clear objective for her business in the long term and how it would work.

It's far too easy to start a business with a general purpose of making more money, but how do you get other people to join your team or advocate for your company when your goal is simply for you to make more money? If making more money easily is what you're after, then you may be better off accepting a lucrative corporate position. Being an entrepreneur is very challenging and not always lucrative.

Keep in mind that the intention of this book is not to discourage people from starting businesses or to focus on failure. Note, as well, that this book is not intended to *prevent* anybody from failing. Failing is part of the learning process. You may have to fail before you get to where you're trying to go. Indeed, failing may be part of your business journey. *The intention of this book is to provide direction toward being strategic in marketing.* Marketing in its entirety is huge, all encompassing, and complicated. It's easy to lose one's way in the marketing maze, and it can be challenging to know where to begin or what to do. So let's start by understanding your main goal.

WHAT IS YOUR CLEAR OBJECTIVE?

Business objectives are the results you hope to achieve and maintain as you run and grow your business. Such objectives may involve profitability, production, and growth. Before you can begin to define detailed business objectives, however, you need to know your main objective, what we call your *clear objective.*

Ultimately, your clear objective should answer this question: **What are you trying to achieve and why are you trying to achieve it?** Take a moment to record your initial response to this vital question, trying to do so in 25 words or less.

____

____

____

____

____

How did you do? Many professionals and entrepreneurs, even those with massive passion for their businesses, find it hard to express concisely their main objectives. Remember, this objective should go beyond merely making money. Perhaps it will be easier to state your main objective once you've considered the remaining keys of Level 1.

Consider that to understand your main objective, it helps to be able to answer fully and succinctly the following questions:

- What is my vision and mission?
- What is my motivation?
- How do I communicate these key business elements?

To answer those questions, we'll examine the powerful keys of bold vision, inspired mission, and reasoned motivation as we continue moving through Level 1.

SETTING YOUR BOLD VISION

Vision is a word that's thrown around a lot these days. Everyone seems to have a vision statement. What, though, does that really mean? Additionally, how does having a bold vision help drive business and marketing success? Moreover, why does one's vision need to be *bold*?

We'd like you to think of your bold vision as a tool for guiding your business toward its goals, and it needs to be bold because it is the core of what sets you apart from your competition in the marketplace. It's fine to have a vision. In fact, it's a must-have. Having a *bold vision*, however, requires you to think beyond the ordinary and everyday, very likely beyond the point at which your competition may be thinking and acting. Even if they are operating at that high level, your bold vision will likely differ from theirs, and differ in a way that sets you apart and offers a unique selling proposition that generates the marketing results you want and need to succeed. Simply, to be a Rockstar Professional, you must think boldly.

It's true that there's an art to writing bold vision statements. Bold vision statements are clear and concise. Writing a clear and concise vision statement is important because it records your vision in print for others to see and understand. Sharing your long-term and short-term goals with others can help inspire others to support you, help you make better business decisions, and hold you accountable for making progress. Having a vision for your company achieves two objectives: it helps you know where you're going and helps your customers know what you stand for and why you're in business. Don't confuse, however, your *bold vision* with your *main objective*. These keys are not the same. Your main objective is what you want above all to achieve. Your vision is the way you see yourself getting there.

RMI POV

Your bold vision provides a common thread that pulls everyone together while providing a picture of the future that pushes you to reach new levels of success.

To clarify, a vision is looking at the big picture. What is your company's vision? Primarily, what are you looking to achieve out of your efforts? Your vision statement should not be vague. An unclear or muddled vision statement can create confusion within a company. Essentially, it leaves people—even the business owner—wondering what's going on within the company and where the company is headed. A clear, concise vision statement should consider the larger scope of where the business is heading and state precise, measurable goals

From Gold Medal Gymnast to Lifestyle Brand

As a 7-time Olympic medalist and the most decorated gymnast in history, Shannon Miller reached the pinnacle of success early in life and is known as the most accomplished gymnast, male or female, in Olympic history. As a standout example of having a bold vision, Shannon has parlayed the drive and ambition needed to become a world-class athlete into a successful brand, Shannon Miller Lifestyle.

Shannon Miller Lifestyle promotes a healthy and balanced lifestyle. Targeted to women, with a focus on health and wellness, it includes the topics of fitness, nutrition, pregnancy, motherhood, cancer awareness, and more. SML reaches out through various partnerships, programs, products, and technologies to educate, motivate, and inspire all women to be their best.

Visit shannonmillerlifestyle.com

ESTABLISHING YOUR INSPIRED MISSION

Perhaps you're beginning to see how the four keys of Level 1 are interconnected. Once you've set your vision, you can now turn your attention to establishing your mission. Your mission statement should guide the actions of your company, spell out its overall goal, provide a clear path, and facilitate smart business decisions, including marketing strategies and tactics. The mission provides the framework or context within which the company's strategies are formulated. It signals what your business is all about to your customers, employees, suppliers, and the community. A mission statement is a tool that can be as important as your business plan.

Think of a company's mission as its guide and framework to follow in order to obtain the vision. It's the *how* the company is going to get there and *what* it stands for. When you understand and state your vision clearly and concisely, you're better prepared to establish business strategies, or pathways, that can fulfill your vision and better able to write an appropriate mission statement.

For example, consider Rock My Image's bold vision: "Ignite your message to amplify business growth and achieve excellence." We've often presented our bold vision in this manner, as well: **I**gnite (your) **M**essage (to) **A**mplify (business) **G**rowth (and achieve) **E**xcellence.

RMI POV

Your inspired mission improves customer and employee engagement with your company, which boosts performance while motivating and inspiring others.

And this way:

IMAGE

IGNITE | MESSAGE | AMPLIFY | GROWTH | EXCELLENCE

Our vision shapes our mission to create first-rate tools and systems needed to empower business owners to reach their goals by leveraging their unique brand and the power of the Internet.

Here's another example, a vision and mission for a nonprofit organization that helps the underserved. The nonprofit's bold vision may be "A world without poverty." Their inspired mission, consequently, may be "Providing jobs for the homeless and unemployed."

Some people may think vision and mission statements are just busy work. These individuals believe that companies put them on their websites and marketing collateral and that nobody cares. This belief is false! When you define the vision of what you're trying to create and why it matters to you, your vision will resonate with people and contribute toward bringing your vision into existence. Likewise, when you state your mission and act upon it, you have a better chance of seeing your vision come true and of others buying into and supporting that vision. These contributors include not only your team members but also potential customers.

Do you need more convincing of the importance of your vision and mission? Consider if you've ever donated to a charity you felt passionate about, or if you've made a purchase because it was for a good cause. Sure you have. People make purchasing decisions all the time because they relate to the company or believe in what the company stands for. Sure, many other factors exist behind our purchasing decisions, but the values and goals of your company play a significant role in moving others to take action, support your cause, or do business with you.

Consider, also, your team members. Do you think people would do a better job if they felt they were contributing to a greater good and vision versus just getting work done? In most cases the answer is yes. If they believe in the company's vision and mission, they will work to help achieve it by playing their part. They may even go above and beyond.

The same can be said about the larger community. Have you witnessed a community support a business that it seemed to value strongly? It happens all the time. When a business has been living a rich and giving mission, the community stands behind it and supports it. *People want to do business with companies that do good.* The values of a company, and "doing good," are communicated through the company's vision and mission.

Even if you're marketing for a company and it's not your business, it is helpful to have a defined vision and mission statement. Do you know the company's vision and mission? If not, investigate these important keys. Then consider if the company's actions and marketing reflect their vision and mission. Also, consider how you can contribute positively to the vision and mission, then take appropriate action.

UNDERSTANDING YOUR REASONED MOTIVATION

Motivation is that force, or energy, that drives you and your business forward. Consider *why* you do what you do. Keep asking *why* until why can't be asked any more. Find the root and let it guide you.

Owning a business is rewarding but also challenging. During the challenging times, you will want to reflect on what we call your "why" to stay motivated. By sharing your why with others, you will inspire them and connect them to you and your brand on a much deeper level.

DISCOVER THE WHY

When marketing a new business, a major challenge is to make others care about your product or service as much as you do, and to turn that caring support into action . . . and by action, we mean *sales*. So, how does an entrepreneur garner support for his or her business? How do you connect with the community and build a following of loyal brand evangelists, social media fans, and happy customers? How do you make people care? How do you stay motivated and inspired in your business?

The answer is that you define *why* you are in business and share it with the world.

People are being marketed to at an astonishing rate. It has been estimated that people are subjected to approximately 2,000 to 3,000 advertisements a day. With so many distractions at our fingertips on our smartphones, laptops, and in the media, it can be very difficult for a business to earn attention for their brand. This is especially difficult if that brand cares more about selling than it does about inspiring. People don't want to be sold to. They want to be inspired. They want to feel like part of a community. They want to buy from businesses that do good. People really do want to make a difference.

In order to earn attention for your business or brand, you must answer the consumer's question, "Why should I care?"

START WITH WHY

Answering the why isn't as difficult or esoteric as it sounds. It is simple, really, because you already know the answer. It's inside of you. You don't need to look to sales pitches, marketing managers, or a list of features and benefits to find the *why*. The why is what motivates you to rise every morning and to do what most people won't. The why is at your core and is the foundation for building a business and brand.

OUR WHY

We speak often to our clients about the importance of understanding their why. We would be remiss if we did not share our own why. We hope it will help you consider your why for taking this journey.

KENNY HARPER

My Why—Leading With Inspiration

Being an inspiring leader ignites my passion.

Throughout life, I've come across people who've influenced me to continue to follow my passion and inspired me to continue to work at it even when I encountered challenges or doubts. Many times, the people who gave me inspiration were not super geniuses, extraordinarily rich, extremely popular, or living their life worry free; they were "normal" people who cared to help.

When I started my career about 15 years ago, I had little direction and little self-confidence. It was a long journey to find some direction and build my confidence to work toward my life goals. Although I had doubts, there was always a deep-rooted faith that I could achieve success if I applied myself. Others inspired me and fueled that faith when I was challenged to continue.

One of my life's missions is to inspire and help others reach their goals. I want to be one of their guiding lights, as others were to me. The world is full of those who need this guidance and insight. I've always felt that helping others find more direction and move further along in their business is incredibly impactful. I realized when I followed this passion that I was excited. It did not feel like work. I'd found my Zen!

Of course, as soon as I found my Zen, the doubt cloud came by to rest above me, which made me stop and question myself. Could I really inspire and lead others? Would people really care what I had to say? After all, I haven't accumulated great riches, produced extremely successful businesses on a large scale, or attained magic answers to questions of success. I'm just an average guy. The business world is replete with resources. Why create something new?

A few key instances have helped to remove the doubt cloud. First, I listened to a goal-planning program where I defined what

I really wanted in life—not the common desires such as money or fame, but what I *really* wanted deep down, the core of what really drives me. After self-reflection it occurred to me that though many things existed that I thought I wanted but didn't have, I already had what I *really* wanted. I was rich and blessed.

I've continued to accomplish the things to which I commit myself. Maybe not to the grandiose level reached by some, but right in line with what I really wanted. I found only cultural perceptions could make me feel as though I needed more when the core of me didn't have that desire.

As I continued with my efforts, I noticed that others, whom I'd not fully acknowledged, were giving me positive feedback. People told me that I'd helped make a difference in their lives. I inspired them. I helped them to see things in a different light, to accomplish more in their lives. I was already doing what I wanted to do. I was giving to the greater good. For whatever reason, although I'd heard people say it, I was minimizing what they were telling me. My eyes were closed, but they were beginning to open.

Finally, I realized that I am rich. I am fulfilling my purpose and passion. There is no need to doubt or question: *Would it be worth it? Would I have anything more to offer?* I can communicate helpful insights and information in my own way with the people I encounter and continue to fulfill my purpose in life. I decided at that point to dedicate applying my knowledge and experience to building my bold vision. I need not worry about all of the details or getting things perfect to get started. I need to set my goals and take action. And that's just what I did.

JEN DeVORE RICHTER

My Why—Freedom

Freedom allows me to live my purpose..

There's a photo my military officer dad has of me at the age of five standing in a tiny version of his military uniform wearing his fatigue green hat. I have my arms crossed across my chest and a smirk on my face that says, *You can't tell me what to do!* That photo is the best representation of who I am at the core. Being a military brat (as we're affectionately called) has given me a wonderful life experience. I was born overseas and have an appreciation for others and their cultures, different ways of life and varying points of view. As a kid, we moved with the Air Force every couple of years, and as an adult, I now find it easy to adapt to new situations, find excitement in travel, and thrive on change.

This upbringing had molded me to be fiercely independent. It's not that I don't depend on others for love, support, and friendship, but I am independent in the sense that I am not afraid to take risks. There is risk involved with starting a business. You risk financial security. You risk being a failure. You risk losing sleep. But to me, the alternative of working for someone else and being told when to be where, what to do, and how to do it, is just not how I want to spend my working life.

I prefer to take risks in business so that I can have freedom. Freedom from the 9 to 5, freedom from overhead fluorescent lights beaming down on my corporate cubicle, freedom from bosses. If I want to travel with my family, I take my laptop with me and can continue to move our business forward. I am accountable to me and my business partners, but because I am free to make my own choices, it doesn't feel like work. We decide how we work, where we work, when we work and with whom. That is a truly liberating feeling! To me, freedom fuels my spirit and is vital to the creative process of building a business.

With this freedom of being a business owner, comes responsibility. We are responsible for everything from the bookkeeping to taking out the office garbage. Because we are responsible for so many aspects of a business, we make many mistakes. What I have learned from my mistakes has been so valuable to both my personal life and career. I've learned to trust my gut more and to not to be afraid to say no. I've learned that perfection isn't attainable and that's OK. Most important, I've learned to ask for help when I don't know something and am on the constant pursuit of progress.

Another important aspect of freedom for me is the ability to define and redefine myself on my terms. I see failures in life or business as an opportunity to reinvent, repurpose and redefine. What a gift it is to be able to take something that is seemingly broken and change it into something new. I probably get this talent from being the "new girl" in school every couple of years when my dad was in the military and we moved. What seemed at the time, a major life challenge has become to me a strength.

Moving forward in my career, I want to continue to inspire others to obtain freedom, especially women. Not just financial freedom, but the personal freedom that can come with being a business owner. It is possible for me to be an attentive wife, a caring "bonus" mom, the favorite aunt, and loving daughter and sister because of my ability to choose when and how I work. With a great support system, a lot of hard work, and a fearless attitude, I can have it all, just not all at the same time. And I'm OK with that.

MANNY TORRES

My Why—Entrepreneurial Spirit

Helping people build their dreams ignites my passion.

The most vivid memories of my childhood involve spending hours playing in my father's knitting factories. There were endless stacks of boxes, huge knitting machines, rolls of cloth, spindles of yarn, and a group of dedicated workers who had become part of our family. It was an impressive operation, and now that I can look back on how my father built it, I'm even more impressed.

My father was born in Puerto Rico and moved to New York City as a teenager. He worked in knitting factories as a mechanic learning the ins and outs of the business. He found a profession he was passionate about and learned as much as he could about the industry. He moved to North Carolina to run a factory and eventually opened his own. Over the years, he's started several businesses, and he strives to provide the highest level of service and the best products for his clients and to create a family atmosphere for his employees. To this day, I am still connected with employees who worked for him over 30 years ago.

In my father's office, hung a painting of a conquistador. A client had given it to him as a gift. My father used an icon of a conquistador as part of his company logo. I always loved the painting. It served as a perfect symbol of the journey my father took, finding his passion, and building a better life for him and his family.

I shared his passion for creating. I had a natural talent for drawing, sparked by my brother, who is a talented artist in his own right. My parents encouraged my talents and I was able to continue with them through school into college and into my first career as a graphic designer. Throughout my career, I've enjoyed helping businesses grow and succeed. I know the sacrifice and struggles business owners encounter. I also know the great opportunities available to those who are determined and persevere through difficulties to build not only a successful business, but also secure their long-term plans.

I look forward to helping aspiring entrepreneurs, business owners, and employees identify what makes them unique and help them showcase that to the world.

GET TO THE CORE

Most people haven't taken the time to consider deeply the core reasons why they do what they do. A lot of people think money drives them but money alone is worthless. Of course, you can buy things with money, but ask yourself if you're working for *things*. Do material objects really drive people? To get to the core, we're going to dig several layers deep into the *why* you really do what you do.

Start by answering simply this question: *Why do you do what you do?* When you answer, ask why again, and repeat the process six times, until you truly find the core.

We got this exercise from Frank DeRaffele (www.frankderaffele.com) who spoke at a Business Networkers International (BNI) conference. He told the story of how he was working with a man who seemed dissatisfied with his life, despite the facts that he had a good paying job, a great family, and many material things. On the surface, he appeared to have it all. In reality, though, he was uninspired, unfulfilled, and unmotivated. Frank asked the man to find his why by asking this series of questions:

When asked Why he did what he did he answered, "To get money."

When asked Why again, he replied, "To be able to afford nice things."

When asked Why again, he replied, "To make my wife and kids happy."

When asked Why again, he replied, "To be a good father and husband."

When asked Why again, he replied, "Because my father was not able to support me."

The core of the reason he worked hard was not to get money; it was to be a better father for his kids than his father was to him. Money has been proven not to buy long-term happiness. Money cannot fuel a fire forever. When you have much more money than you'd ever need, what would be your motivation then? Finding the true reason for his efforts gave him something to which he could stay passionate and committed.

The same can be said for the why behind starting a business. The reasons why you do what you do affects many factors that can contribute to your potential for success.

Try this "why" exercise now:

Why do you do what you do?

____

Why?

____

Why?

____

Why?

____

Why?

____

Why?

____

Why?

So what's the real reason? What is that inner passion pushing you? How can you share it with the world and in your marketing?

LEVEL 1 AMPLIFIERS AND TWEAKS

AMPLIFIERS

1. Write down the vision and mission for your life and business so you can begin to identify your purpose.
2. Write down your purpose, passion, and gifts. Refer to the introduction for definitions of these concepts.
3. Revisit your vision and mission and check that it aligns with your purpose, passion, and gifts.

TWEAKS

1. If you're feeling frustrated by lackluster marketing results, get back on track by realigning your business focus to your mission and vision.
2. If you're feeling uninspired, get energized by remembering your motivation and reminding yourself of your passion, purpose, and gifts.

LEVEL 1 DIALERS AND DRAINERS

DIALERS

1. Surround yourself with other people that have positive attitudes. They will help keep you energized.
2. Listen to motivational podcasts and audiobooks to keep your mindset focused.
3. Make time for family, friends, hobbies, and rest to recharge.

DRAINERS

1. Beware of mismatched clients and projects that may distract you from your purpose and drain your passion. Short-term gain can detract from your long-term goals, if not in alignment.
2. Avoid saying yes to every marketing opportunity that comes along. Pause and ask yourself if the marketing in question helps you realize your vision and achieve your mission.

Battle with Cancer Inspires Business

When Jim Borngesser battled cancer in 2013, he and his wife, Anne, stayed at a friend's apartment for his postsurgical recovery from his extensive procedures at New York's Memorial Sloan Kettering Cancer Center. As part of his treatment process, Jim received home visits from a medical practitioner. Depending on someone else to assist with the daily living tasks freed Anne up to focus on being Jim's emotional support. This made such a huge difference for Jim and his family. He pondered the questions of how to care for the whole family during health challenges and how to celebrate life.

Over a year after being declared cancer free, Jim was inspired to launch Family Focused Home Health Care. Family Focused Home Health Care provides a continuum of nonmedical, in-home care to seniors and others. The company name is their inspired mission and expressed not just in concept but also in the attitudes of their caregivers, the quality of their services, and the way they care for their clients.

SHARPENING YOUR AWARENESS

You Are Your Story

No rock star makes it to the big time without understanding himself or herself as an artist. Those who hit it big, and stay relevant, are clear on their objective, vision, and mission. Their passion fuels them. They're clear on their motivation. They're willing to put in the hours it takes to achieve their objective, to realize their vision. What may look like an overnight success is rarely such. The Rockstar Professional's sharp self-awareness and awareness of their competitors, others who strive for their audience's attention and spending capital, propels him or her through Level 2, to greater gains. Level 2 is not to be dismissed easily; Level 2 is where we gain clarity about our competitors and ourselves, and where we learn about the 4 Competition Truths.

THE LEVEL 2 GAINS: THE 5 CHORDS OF BRANDING YOURSELF

- Understanding your core competencies
- Crafting your story
- Identifying your unique selling proposition
- Connecting with your audience
- Upping your game

LEVEL 2 KEY TERMS

Authority Marketing. Marketing that frames the professional as the expert in his or her field in an effort to gain and retain customers.

Content Marketing. A strategic marketing approach focused on creating and distributing original, relevant, and consistent content to attract and retain a clearly-defined audience and, ultimately, to drive profitable customer action.

Competitor. A business in the same goods or services market as yours and has the same customer base.

Core Competencies. A body of knowledge or set of skills that allows a business to achieve a high level of success.

Unique Selling Proposition. What makes you different, *and better*, than your competitors, what gives you an advantage over your competition.

LEVEL 2 SELF-ASSESSMENT

Answer the following yes/no questions to gauge your current Level 2 readiness achievement:

1. I recognize that *all* businesses have competition, even those based on the most original ideas.
2. I know who my top three competitors (T3C) are and understand what makes each unique.
3. My business has a unique way of engaging with customers, delivering services, or providing a solution.

If you answered yes to all three questions, that's fantastic. Now, prepare yourself to delve into Level 2 and understand even better yourself and your competitors. If you did not answer yes to each question, now is your opportunity to understand on a deep level yourself, your business, and your competitors. Your business fellows are sharpening their awareness of themselves and *you* every day. The Rockstar Professional will do likewise.

UNDERSTANDING YOUR CORE COMPETENCIES

We call the gains of Level 2 "chords" because to strike it big in marketing you need to strike the right chords, all 5 of them. To do so, you must first recognize that you have certain core competencies. These competencies are with you already. You possess a body of knowledge and a set of skills that are preparing you for success in your business, as the company owner or an employed professional of someone else's business.

RMI POV

Identifying your company values is one of the first action items, as it will help you make better decisions in all areas of your business but especially in hiring your team, aligning with partners, and taking on clients. If people don't have your values, then you should think twice about aligning with them.

Unfortunately, some in business—perhaps in business for years—don't possess a clear understanding of their core competencies. They haven't examined and accepted their passion, purpose, and gifts. Furthermore, they haven't assessed what they know and can do and what they *don't know* and *can't do*. These professionals haven't acknowledged their strengths and weaknesses—much less the strengths and weaknesses of their competitors. It's a basic truth that you have a set of core competencies. Now, the question is, how do you come to discover these?

KNOW YOUR VALUES AND BELIEFS

By knowing and defining your values and beliefs, you can help to make important decisions that align with your values and to attract and include people with likeminded beliefs. Not everybody who helps to market your product or service needs to have the exact same values and beliefs you hold, although the more people who share your values, the better the chance that they will follow a plan that adheres to your values. If you don't clearly define your values, you leave the door open for values and attitudes that don't reflect you to find their way into your business, brand, and marketing.

LEAD WITH YOUR VALUES

Defining the values that create your culture can help set the tone of your communications as well. Examine the list of values below that can ensure people operate "above the line" and with good ethics:

- Abundance
- Balance
- Commitment
- Communication
- Consistency
- Excellence
- Gratitude
- Integrity
- Ownership
- Success
- Teamwork

When a marketing team works together on a marketing plan, they should utilize the shared values defined in both the creation and execution of the marketing efforts. While it's much easier to create a list than to follow it, having the list defined is the first step toward ensuring the desired values are being recognized and enforced.

Values transcend our business life and find their way into our personal lives. Likewise, our personal lives can provide a template for the values we hold in business. The Rockstar Professional finds himself or herself in balance and alignment with his or her core value system. The Rockstar doesn't worry about thinking and behaving one way in his or her personal life and another way in his or her business life. The RP understands and acts upon his or her core value system.

RECORD YOUR VALUES

It seems a given that businesses who take the time to understand their core values would also take the time to record those values in written form. Writing and publishing your values makes it clear who you are, provided that you act in accordance with those values.

At Rock My Image, our values represent the core of who we really are:

- Trustworthy and integrity-filled reputations that help build our brand and business
- Passionate spirits that keep us motivated and inspire others
- Positive attitudes about our work and lives
- Bold visions for our future and current success, as well as for our clients
- Creative minds to produce great work
- Results-oriented actions for a more effective approach
- Fun, playful environments that make coming to work and working with us a joy

- Smart people so that we can learn from each other
- Leadership abilities to grow in our careers, lead by example, and teach others

At Rock My Image, we only work with and for people that share our values.

KEEP IN CHECK WITH YOUR VALUES

You may be able to sell more products and services, at least in the short run, by using deceit and deception, making false claims, and being obstructive. For decades, companies have swindled people out of their hard-earned money. How many commercials have you watched where a company makes amazing claims about its product, convincing you to buy; then, when you get the product, you're left disappointed? We've all been there at some time. These companies don't care. They've made their money and are off to the next "sucker." Obviously, this is not the path to long-term success, as eventually word of mouth helps reveal the truth—and the company's core values.

If you're marketing a company, you may be persuaded to try some marketing tactics that trick consumers to take action and purchase your product. Someone may even try to convince you it's not a bad tactic. This would be a good time to review your values; if the tactic is counter to your values, you should probably avoid it. You can't create advocates and raving fans of your company by tricking people. It just doesn't work that way.

CHECK YOUR ATTITUDE, TOO

As business and marketing professionals, we can have the most stellar value system in place, in theory; if we don't keep our attitude in check, though, are we really honoring it? It's vital to our success to check our attitude, too.

Do you have and keep a healthy attitude? While we can't expect to have our expectations met 100 percent of the time, we should be able to keep the right mindset a majority of the time. A negative or doubtful attitude can easily affect one's judgement and degrade the full potential of a marketing effort.

Let's consider, for example, this fictional scenario based on our actual experience:

Nancy opened Goo-Goo, a new children's entertainment establishment, and hired Barbara, a social media marketer, to help her get the word out about her store. The owner was reluctant to hire her and didn't understand how making posts on social media was going to help grow her business, so she saw the social media marketer as an expense rather than an investment. Initially, Barbara created interesting posts that were unique and engaging, but a disappointed Nancy was quick to point out that the engagement did not lead to immediate store foot traffic. Nancy wanted the social media posts to be more sales related and only focus on getting people to come to Goo-Goo. After Nancy complained to Barbara several times, Barbara was no longer excited about the campaign and from that point forward posted only stale "salesy" posts. After another month of the campaign, Nancy saw the social engagement go down and canceled the campaign. She knew it wasn't going to work after all.

This scenario has repeated itself far too many times throughout the course of marketing. A doubting, controlling, negative attitude made a self-fulfilling prophesy and essentially created its own failure. Remember these key points based on Nancy's failure:

- If you're part of a team, be part of the team.
- Be optimistic and learn from any mistakes.
- Keep an open mind and trust qualified people to make decisions.

If you're determined something will fail, it's more likely to fail. If you're determined for something to succeed, it can succeed, given a period of trial and error. Be aware of turning your negative thoughts into negative words. We truly can speak our success or failure into reality.

Checking our attitude is often about managing our expectations. What are your expectations when it comes to marketing? Do you want immediate, quick results, or are you willing to work for long-term success? These are important questions because if you go into marketing with the wrong expectations, you may end up disappointed and lose the vigor to be successful.

It's been stated that *marketing is math*. While that statement contains truth, marketing is also *trial and error*. You must try different marketing strategies, measure to evaluate what works and what doesn't, and work to refine the strategies to achieve better results over time. If you expect to try some marketing strategies and measure results right away, you could potentially eliminate profitable marketing strategies that take more time to cultivate. Maybe we should declare that *marketing is time*. The

Rockstar Professional knows that marketing is all these things, and perhaps it's best stated that *marketing is an art.*

ACKNOWLEDGE YOUR KNOWLEDGE BASE

So we know our core values, and we've checked in with our values and our attitudes. Now what? Now we take an honest look at our knowledge base. Are we experienced and qualified to make marketing decisions? Is our team experienced and qualified to do so? Is there perhaps a better way to market than the do-it-yourself approach we may be taking?

Similar to the previous example of Nancy, too many times people make marketing decisions based on emotion or personal preferences and not on experience, data, or an understanding of marketing. An abundant amount of information and marketing knowledge is available online. Research goes a long way to provide key information that can help us make decisions that are more informed and to improve the possibilities for success with our marketing efforts.

If you're a business owner or entrepreneur with little marketing knowledge, listen to the advice of experienced, proven marketers, or prove your case on why your opposing rationale would be a better choice. Don't hinder the process by letting your emotions or preference control the process. Rockstar Professionals don't get in their own way. If you have marketing knowledge, don't be too quick to think you have all the answers. The musician who knows a *little bit* about electricity should not be the one in charge of rewiring the stage.

On the flipside, if you're the marketer assisting a business owner or entrepreneur, you may be the one who's challenged to keep your strategy. In this case, you should attempt to persuade the business owner your strategy is the right move through education and data. In some cases, you may help them to understand and yet they may remain determined to do things their way, regardless of how many professionals try to help them. Pick your battles. If it's something small, you may choose to let them have their way and let it go. If it's something profound, you may refuse to do it and hold your ground. While you may lose business this way, it may help you keep your integrity. For example, we would not help someone market blatant lies, no matter how much the client might pay. It goes against our core ethical values.

The bottom line is to educate yourself on the key elements of marketing and trust the experience of your team or colleagues to make important marketing decisions. By knowing yourself and understanding your core competencies, you can evaluate better how you play into the roles and decisions of marketing efforts.

CRAFTING YOUR STORY

We've titled Level 2 "You Are Your Story" because it's true. You *are* your branded "story." Our love of story, in fact, is hardwired into our human brains. When we hear a story, all the regions of our brain activate as if we're experiencing the event ourselves. Leo Widrich, cofounder of Buffer, published a fascinating article on the power of storytelling on Lifehacker.com.[2] Widrich makes a

RMI POV

Every business has a story. Yes, even *yours!* Maximize and communicate your story so that you differentiate yourself from your competitors.

compelling argument in favor of steering away from multiple lists and bullet points in posts and moving toward storytelling to capture and engage readers. The same case can be made for engaging customers and capturing market share. Storytelling works, and it's too often passed over as "wordy" or "unsophisticated." The right story told simply and genuinely can have a profound effect on communicating who you are and connecting with customers who want to know you and your brand.

The story you communicate as a professional or business encapsulates your brand. Branding is the first pillar of marketing and a crucial part of the success of all marketing efforts, as every marketing effort falls back on the strength of the branding. The 3 Pillars of Marketing will be examined thoroughly in volume 2 of the AMP series. What's important to recognize now is that while you're building your brand, you're also crafting your story. Your story is part of your brand, whether it's a personal brand or a company brand, and it's part of how you're remembered in others' minds.

Let's examine a few classic "story" types. Are you the small-town kid who found major success in the big city? Are you the nose-to-the-grindstone scholar who had a big idea and took a risk to find success? Did your company start out in a cramped garage with a few dollars and tons of gumption to strike it rich in your market? Maybe these archetypal brand stories reminded you of actual professionals or companies. The small-town kid could be Jackie Robinson or Taylor Swift; the scholar with the big idea, former New Jersey senator, NBA player, and Rhodes Scholar Bill Bradley; and the company with humble beginnings just about any now-rich Silicon Valley startup, including Apple, Google, and Amazon.

Your story stays with you, so it's vital to get your story straight. Your story and how you want to be known sets the tone for your brand. It establishes your beginnings and defines who you are, your core values, your vision and mission, and your motivation. It's important to note one difference between branding and your story is that while branding is a living, breathing effort that can evolve and be refined, your story is mostly fixed and, once established, rarely changes. It's good, therefore, to be mindful of how you want to be known to the world. It's also important to know that awareness and sharing of your branded story can lead to identifying and promoting your unique selling proposition.

IDENTIFYING YOUR UNIQUE SELLING PROPOSITION OR YOUR CLAIM TO FAME

We encourage you to appreciate, celebrate, and market your unique selling proposition (USP). Recognizing your USP is what gives you an advantage over your competitors, a crucial aspect of Level 2 gains, and it's not mere lip service. Think of your USP as your "claim to fame." In a sentence, your USP should complete this thought: *We are the only company that. . . .*

We invite you now to complete this thought for yourself:

We are the only company that

____

____

____

____

How did you do? Some businesses struggle to state succinctly their unique selling proposition. Consider that your USP may extend from various factors. Here are a few:

- Your written guarantee
- Your proven, unique process
- Your secret formula or recipe
- Your pricing structure
- Your placement strategy (a unique selling location or means of distribution)
- Product characteristics that solve an unsolved problem
- Certifications or awards

Consider that your USP must be strong enough to move others to action. It has to include a specific benefit in the mind of the consumer, not just advertising "fluff" or showmanship.

As an example, here is the RMI USP:

RMI'S CLAIM TO FAME

- Developers of the Rock My Image Action Marketing Platform (AMP)™ proven approach and the RMI Authority Marketing Tracker and Scorecard™
- Authors of *Amplify Your Business: A Rockstar Professional's Guide to Marketing Success, Volume 1*

Beyond claims, you can combine the USP with tangible outcomes and real results that you've achieved for existing clients.

RMI'S USP PLUS REAL RESULT

Rock My Image is the developer of the unique and proven approach Action Marketing Platform (AMP)™ system. A current client, a physician and owner of a regional vein center, experienced year-over-year increases of 140 percent in converted online ad clicks, 83 percent increase in website traffic, and a 35 percent increase in contact forms, helping him to grow from one location to four in just two years without a significant increase in his advertising budget.

Another Rock My Image client, a plastic surgeon, experienced year-over-year increases

RMI POV

A unique presence in a crowded marketplace is instrumental to gaining an edge over your competition. Don't be afraid to speak up, stand out, and outshine!

of 90 percent in converted ad clicks, 105 percent in website visits, and a 332 percent increase in contact forms, radically improving revenue and sales without a significant increase in advertising budget.

REVEAL YOUR USP THROUGH A SWOT ANALYSIS

We understand that recognizing your USP may not come as easily as completing a sentence starter. It may take deep introspection and the assistance of marketing professionals. One of our first steps with new clients is to perform a SWOT analysis to help them identify their unique selling proposition. Most professionals these days are familiar with a SWOT analysis, which stands for strengths, weaknesses, opportunities, and threats. The portion of the analysis that helps most in identifying a business's USP is an exploration of its strengths. In other words, it reveals what you're doing better than your competition, thus helping you identify your USP. Remember that although you may feel a rush to start marketing, a SWOT analysis is not a step to be skipped.

Competing for market share is one of the biggest challenges in marketing. If there were already high demand for your product and absolutely no competition against it, then marketing would be as easy as establishing awareness. The fact that great competition usually exists means you must be competitive. You must exceed the competition in some way. You must gain an edge and communicate your unique selling proposition.

Keep in mind this truism: *In business, being good is not good enough.*

In today's market, providing a decent product with good customer service is expected and is not something that distinguishes you against your competition. Most direct competitors offer comparable quality and service, so you'll need to find something else to place you center stage.

To see this in action, we can look at the music industry. The most successful, iconic performers have something that's unique and original. They don't just say they're different. They *are* different, and they stand out from the sea of sameness. When success is achieved because of originality, the artist will influence other acts; in turn, their musical sound, entertainment quality, style, or showmanship will begin to slowly influence other musicians. Once that happens, the originality becomes muddled, but you can't deny the lead act that introduced a new sound or performance style. As time passes, new stars emerge offering a unique sound or approach and the cycle continues.

When considering marketing, your USP, and your competition, consider the words of Sun Tzu, Chinese general and philosopher, credited as the author of *The Art of War:* "Know thyself, know thy enemy. A thousand battles, a thousand victories." You may have a smaller battle to fight than does the recording artist trying to sell a million gold records or win a Grammy. Your battle, though, is just as important.

If you're selling a consumer good with a low price and you're in a prime location, you may not have a large challenge. For example, an ice cream shop at the beach with no other similar vendors close to the location may have high demand and low competition. Focusing on awareness and customer loyalty may be enough to be successful in business in that location. Growing the company, however, to new locations may require more thought and effort. In fact, it takes a Rockstar Professional who has branded the company's story and is consistently communicating the company's USP to edge out the competition in new locations. The RP ice cream shop owner knows her unique selling proposition: a better-tasting ice cream with a twist, ingredients her competition doesn't use, and awesome flavors they don't offer.

USING SWOT ANALYSIS TO CONTINUALLY DEFINE AND COMMUNICATE YOUR USP

Once you've defined your SWOT and you understand your place in the landscape of competition, including your unique selling proposition, you can begin to develop a plan to take advantage of the insights. This may be painfully obvious at this point; however, we continually find most people don't take the time to go fully through this process. This exercise should be coordinated on a regular basis since things change constantly. We cannot stress enough that defining and communicating your USP is an ongoing marketing process, one that continues to amp up your marketing energy. Once you've identified your USP and gained insights through a SWOT analysis, it's time to add marketing action to your analysis.

Communicate Your Strengths: If you have strengths against your competition, you need to communicate these clearly both internally to your employees and, of course, externally to your customers.

Strengthen Your Weaknesses: Continual improvement of and attention to your weaknesses is necessary to maintain a competitive edge and customer satisfaction.

Leverage Your Opportunities: If you have unique opportunities that have not been offered to your competition or are due to circumstances you created to obtain an edge, don't waste these moments, leverage them!

Check Your Threats: Always be aware of changes in your industry, new competition in your market, and other internal or external threats that could bring your competitive edge down.

LEARN HOW SMALL THINGS MAKE A BIG DIFFERENCE

Have you ever noticed the way in which the smallest little things can make the biggest difference? In his book *Purple Goldfish*, Stan Phelps discusses and shares many examples of marketing lagniappe (pronounced lan-yap). *Lagniappe* refers to the little unexpected extras given free that are relevant and valued by the consumer. The goal here is to create a differentiator, give an experience, and create a memory that can win continued business or even, in some cases, be shared by word of mouth or social media.

A restaurant that offers free bread or chips and salsa with a meal.

> An automobile oil change business that vacuums the inside of each customer's car as a complimentary service.
>
> A high-end hotel that offers complimentary champagne upon check-in.
>
> The local yoga studio that provides each student with a lavender-scented, chilled cloth at the end of each class.
>
> A cosmetic surgeon's office that offers valet parking to her patients.

If you find that you're not offering lagniappe now, take a few moments to brainstorm three ideas that you can easily and affordably implement. This can help distinguish you further and help grow your business organically. Keep in mind that you don't have to give away money. Brainstorm other ways to include lagniappe:

- Give an experience.
- Make things easier.
- Provide special treatment.

Try brainstorming lagniappe ideas now. How many can you imagine?

____

____

____

____

____

LET YOUR USP AND SWOT ANALYSIS DRIVE YOUR MARKETING

Marketing and advertising can help get your message in front of potential customers, but it can't force them to choose you. If your competition has an edge over you because of its unique selling proposition, you'll be facing an uphill battle trying to convince people to choose you. Spending more money in marketing may only result in mediocre results and having a higher than desired customer churn rate. In addition to marketing your business, focus on building a better product, providing a more unique service, and playing to your strengths to achieve better results.

RMI POV

Amplified marketing provides a channel for connecting with your audience in a natural, organic fashion. It's less "salesy" and in step with the modern buyer's journey.

CONNECTING WITH YOUR AUDIENCE

Rock stars know about connecting with their audiences. Most are in front of their audiences on a consistent basis, at least those who continue to be relevant and profitable. Whether it's a live concert, a talk show, a print interview, or their personal websites, they're constantly connecting with their target market. You're gaining marketing energy and becoming a Rockstar Professional, so you bet it's paramount that you, at the very least, start considering ways to connect with your audience.

You'll recall that part of Rock My Image's unique selling proposition is that we get our clients in front of their audiences in a way that grow and nurture their fan bases. We do that better than our competition, through two marketing vehicles: *authority marketing* and *content marketing*.

UNDERSTAND AUTHORITY MARKETING

Authority marketing is positioning yourself as an expert in your industry in order to gain visibility and credibility for your company. To position yourself as an expert, you must first actually *be* an expert. Second, you must be willing to step into the spotlight and enjoy the notoriety—and the criticism— that comes from being in the limelight. Third, you must be willing to share your knowledge and experience in a helpful, educational, and entertaining way that is not "salesy."

As business marketer, you're probably behaving in traditional ways to get attention for your company. This might be running TV ads, running print ads, passing out brochures at events, and attending trade shows. All these marketing tactics have value, but if you're looking for a new way, a different way of elevating your business, let's look closer at marketing with authority. We help position our clients as authorities in their markets in part because it provides desired audience exposure in an authentic, meaningful way that highlights our clients' unique selling propositions. What this positioning as *the* authority means for our clients is a magnified return on investment, greater reach, richer results, and more freedom.

MAKE THE AUTHORITY MARKETING-CONTENT MARKETING CONNECTION

At this point, you may have accepted the need for and value of authority marketing. Still, though, you may be standing on your "business stage" scratching your head, wondering, *How do I convince my audience that I'm the authority they know, like, and trust?* At Rock My Image, we're experts at making the Authority Marketing-Content Marketing Connection. We help our clients express their knowledge base—in essence, their authority—through strategic content marketing tactics. We assist them in using their knowledge base to generate relevant, dynamic content that speaks to their audience. We help ignite their audience's passion for their products and services. Three ways we do this that generate a massive amount of marketing energy is through social media, email marketing, and video content.

CREATE "STICKY" CONTENT FOR SOCIAL MEDIA

Once we've created website content in the form of PDFs or white papers or even blog posts, this provides fantastic information and content to share on your social media accounts. We create content in a way that sticks with your audience. Granted, most companies today have social media accounts; some post regularly to these accounts and some don't. Most, however, are missing the point of posting their content. *Content has to stick in the consumers' minds!* We understand the formula for generating sticky content, much of which comes down to crafting a simple but unexpected and emotional story. We're pros at social media and the widgets and software programs that can push this sticky content automatically to your social media accounts.

Some companies, however, are invested in the DIY-model of marketing. If you're such a company and generating your own content for your website or blog, you may be able to install the right widgets and software programs onto your website yourself or have your marketing manager do it. Be sure, though, that you're pushing your content out regularly and that the content has that sticky factor; otherwise, your efforts may not yield the results you need. Remember that one purpose for posting content to social media is to pull those following you on social media to your website. That's a big part of the Authority Marketing-Content Marketing Connection. Great content pulls people to your website, where you really shine as an authority.

The Rockstar Professional, though, will often find that he or she is too busy with new business to turn their knowledge base into the right content marketing that makes the Authority Marketing-Content Marketing Connection, which is why they come to an authority-savvy marketing agency such as RMI. The RP has moved beyond the DIY marketing model.

KEEP "TOP OF MIND" WITH EMAIL MARKETING

Email marketing is not new. Ask yourself this question, though: Are you using email marketing effectively as a burgeoning

Rockstar Professional? Do you have a regular e-newsletter system in place to disseminate your sticky content you've created on your website and blog? Instead of a standard newsletter, one disconnected from your website and blog, your RP e-newsletter should mirror the content posted on your website and blog.

When we put in place the systems and tools to acquire, nurture, convert, and retain (ANCR) your fan base (i.e., your loyal customers), we ensure your content has focus on a monthly, quarterly, and annual basis. We'll examine the power of ANCR thoroughly in Volume 2 of the AMP™ series, but, for now, let's stay focused on email marketing. Again, the do-it-yourself email marketing model works for some, but often it can become a mishmash of so-so content. The Rockstar Professional is not happy with weak content. *Weak content, weak results!* The RP has too much knowledge base to settle for anything less than stellar content. If you're creating your own content, ensure your blog post topics on your website correspond to topics presented in your newsletter and vice versa. Likewise, embed links into your newsletter that link back to your blog and website.

CONNECT WITH VIDEO

Video is an incredible way to connect with your audience. With video, your fan base relates to you and sees you as the expert. Humans are highly visual creatures. The primary visual cortex, that part of our brain that receives and processes sensory nerve impulses from the eyes, spans over 20 percent of the surface area of the neocortex.[3] What does that factoid mean to you? Simply put, if you're going to connect with your audience and engage their brains, you need highly visual content. You need video content.

For years, top brands have been posting record numbers of video content on YouTube and other video-sharing sites. And, they've gotten really good at it! They know they must integrate their video content on their sharing sites, such as their YouTube accounts, with their websites. They know how to create video content that people want to share, that they feel compelled to share. We create that level of video content for our RP clients. If you're still on the DIY model, though, remember to link your video content to your website, blog, e-newsletter, and social media.

UPPING YOUR GAME

Once you've identified your unique selling proposition and positioned yourself as an authority through content marketing, you're ready to advance in Level 2 by what many call *upping your game*. When will you know it's time to raise your game? In cutthroat industries, it may be super competitive to win business, and you must "up your game" just to get attention. Companies that sell large-ticket items with many competing alternatives must be creative and clear on the reasons buyers should choose them. For example, car dealers, medical practices, and financial advisors need to market their services aggressively as multiple options exist for consumers in those markets. If this is your business type, you'll likely need to up your game regularly just to stay competitive.

Let us state with conviction that the Rockstar Professional focuses on upping his or her game *regularly and with passion*! Doing so drives the realization of the bold vision and inspired mission the RP set in Level 1.

RMI POV

Marketing should be a reflection of what your business is truly about and how you operate. RMI considers it an extension of your customer experience. Are you aware of the numerous ways a prospect interacts with your brand before, during, and after the sale? What do those interactions say about you?

WAYS TO UP YOUR GAME

It's easy to say, *OK, it's time for me to up my game.* Doing so, in reality, may seem daunting, but it need not be. We've created a memorable way to think about and act on upping your game, using the noun *game* itself.

Up Your GAME

G – Give

A – Associate

M – Manage

E – Elevate

GIVE: Our business and personal lives keep us busy, but we must guard against becoming too busy to consider the ways that giving can up our game. Too often business professionals and owners have a what-can-I-*get* mentality. Try nurturing a what-can-I-*give* mentality—in an open and genuine, not manipulative way—and see how those efforts turn into organic marketing opportunities. Particularly in networking situations, come with a what-can-I-give attitude and you'll see that more people will want to connect with you. Be smart about your giving, though, it's not about how much you can give (you'll wear yourself and your company out), but how you can give in well-considered, meaningful ways that result in growing yourself and your business.

ASSOCIATE: We associate with others on a daily basis. When we stop to reflect upon those with whom we associate, are they positive, energy-infusing people, or are they negative, energy-draining people? With whom and what we associate matters—who we're connected to, what we're associated with. You can up your game by being thoughtful about your associations and developing ones that are more meaningful.

MANAGE: It's the classic struggle: how to manage our lives well. By lives, we include our time, relationships, business dealings, basically everything. We recommend evaluating how you're managing all aspects of your life, on at least a quarterly basis, if not weekly or even daily. When we manage our lives well, it leaves us more time to concentrate on forming and executing smart marketing strategies. A chaotic life cannot support a healthy, growing business.

ELEVATE: A well-managed life will naturally lead to wanting to elevate ourselves and our businesses. Elevating is about lifelong learning, not settling for mediocrity, and making the most out of our strengths and opportunities while shoring up our weaknesses and minimizing threats. It's not about being unsettled or dissatisfied with our businesses or ourselves, but about accepting where our business and we as individuals are and continuing to grow from that point forward. If you'll recall the section "Check Your Attitude, Too" earlier in this level, elevating our businesses and ourselves is inextricably tied to our attitudes. The Rockstar Professional cultivates an attitude of consistent elevation.

Now, up your GAME. In five minutes, note as many ways you can think of to give, associate, manage, and elevate your business or yourself as a business professional or company owner. We bet you'll surprise yourself with what you're able to brainstorm.

WAYS TO UP MY GAME:

Give:

____

____

____

____

Associate:

____

____

____

____

Manage:

____

____

____

____

Elevate:

____

____

____

____

We hope you came up with some awesome ways to up your game. Remember, though, that the RP will develop a marketing action plan (MAP), a keyword being *action*, in Level 3. To see results, you'll need to put your good ideas into action.

Being Unique Brings Big Gains

In 2008, Jason Zook had an idea that was crazy enough to be genius. He realized that he could get paid to wear T-shirts on social media. As sites such as Facebook, Twitter, YouTube, Ustream, and Flickr grew in popularity, he saw the need for companies to be able to maximize exposure in unique and creative ways. So, each day he represented a different company online by wearing their T-shirt and creating interesting content around the brand.

In 2013 and 2014, he auctioned off his last name to the highest bidders and was paid to be known as Jason HeadsetsDotCom, Jason SurfrApp and now Jason Zook. He also wrote his first book, Creativity for Sale, which he self-published by crowdsourcing over $75,000 worth of sponsorships on the bottom of each page of the book.

Jason now helps entrepreneurs take a leap of faith through a variety of projects, including his Action Army podcast. While his platform may change, one thing remains the same: you can always count on Jason Zook to "up his game."

Visit jasondoesstuff.com

BE AWESOME INSIDE AND OUT

You'll notice that we used the word *awesome* in reference to upping one's game. At Rock My Image, we believe in the power of awesomeness. What does it mean to be awesome? Let's start with the dictionary definition, according to OxfordDictionaries.com:

awe•some
ˈôsəm/
adjective
extremely impressive or daunting
inspiring great admiration, apprehension, or fear.
«the awesome power of the atomic bomb»

synonyms: breathtaking, awe-inspiring, magnificent, wonderful, amazing, stunning, staggering, imposing, stirring, impressive

antonyms: unimpressive

informal: extremely good; excellent.
"the band is truly awesome!"

In our discussion, though, the word *awesome* means much more. It means you not only "talk the talk" but also you "walk the walk."

The saying "a chain is only as strong as its weakest link" holds true in many instances. It definitely holds true when it comes to marketing. If you want to *own it*, you need to *rock it*. You need to be awesome both inside and outside, from your product and brand to your image and service, as well as everything in between. You'll lose wherever you're weak, so you must be *awesome from the inside out*.

To illustrate this point, consider the car manufacturer Lexus. In 1989, Lexus launched a marketing campaign that communicated their values: The Relentless Pursuit of Perfection. While Lexus knew that perfection actually could not be obtained, they coined the "relentless pursuit of perfection," assuring people that they would go above and beyond to strive for the absolute best. Likewise, they operated their business with that core model in mind.

You may not be as relentless as Lexus striving for perfection, but you should at least strive for continual improvement on the way to becoming awesome. If you're trying to beat the competition with a "good enough" approach, then you might as well just cut them a check and throw in the towel. "Good enough" isn't going to cut it.

If you're reading this book, it's safe to assume that you're looking to be awesome. You're looking to rock. Or, at the very least, you want awesome results; you want to reach your dreams. Moving through the sections of Level 2 and putting the ideas presented in this level into action will put you on the road to awesome and closer to Level 11: Rockstar Professional.

So why be awesome? In order to reach a level of success where the business is growing itself, it's helpful if something about the business is truly awesome. Sure, plenty of examples exist where brands that could be categorized as "OK" have done very well. These brands, however, are in danger of being replaced, if an alternative solution proves to be a better value. There are even more examples of companies that once dominated an industry and looked untouchable but eventually lost out, as they could not compete with the up-and-coming competition.

WHAT TO KEEP IN MIND ABOUT BEING AWESOME

Even though we suggest striving for awesomeness, and we believe being awesome is possible, keep in mind the following points:

Perfection is not obtainable: You shouldn't aim for things to be perfect. If so, you'll fail every time. Remember, nothing is perfect. What may seem perfect for one may seem awful to the next, so it's only a fallacy to obtain perfection. Instead, work toward improvement or a continual effort toward making things better and keeping things fresh. Don't lose your edge.

Being awesome is in the eye of the beholder: As we mentioned above, people view, experience, and judge things differently. Therefore, know your audience and know what your audience likes. You can't please everyone. In many cases, the more you try to please everyone, the less likely you'll be awesome to anyone. You only need to be awesome to the audience you're targeting.

If it's not broken, don't fix it: This is another common saying packed with truth; however, it's not 100 percent accurate. Think about it; many things throughout time that weren't broken have been improved. Think if the airplane that the Wright brothers crafted or the Ford Model A had never been improved because they "worked." Some things may not need to be tweaked or fixed. Sometimes people create something fantastic and changing it doesn't help. Yet, sometimes these changes do help. If you don't try, you won't know, and then you can't learn from it.

LISTEN TO YOUR CUSTOMERS, BUT BE OPEN TO CHANGE

More can be said about not tampering with an already great product. Recall Coca-Cola's bad call in the 1980s when they came out with a new formula for Coke? This was a real business blunder. Coke lost market share trying to fix something that people already liked. The American public's reaction to the change was extremely negative. The company eventually reintroduced their original formula, rebranding it as "Coca-Cola Classic" and achieving significant gain in sales. This may have hurt Coca-Cola in the short term, but it actually helped them in the long term. Had they not tried the change, they would not have gained the knowledge and the positive results from the experience.

Changes can be risky. With risk, however, comes reward. Stay open to change, and remember that each instance of making changes should be evaluated to determine the risk and potential reward. Take action, learn, and gain from the experience, or take no action and wonder what could have happened. These 3 points about being awesome should keep you moving through the 10 levels that lead to Level 11 and becoming a Rockstar Professional.

A QUICK AND EASY AWESOMENESS ASSESSMENT

Below are three main areas where you can perform a quick, easy assessment of your awesomeness that will relate to your marketing. We've designed it as an outline so that you can complete the outline and your own rocking awesomeness plan!

1. The Product
    a. Core problem it solves
    b. Features
    c. Benefits

2. The Brand
    a. Company culture
    b. Communication style
    c. Company values

3. The Funnel
    a. Marketing
    b. Sales
    c. Customer touchpoints

Of course, this is a simplified assessment of a brand, and you should consider and evaluate many other aspects of marketing and your business, but these elements are the key points to focus on, demanding your attention first. In summary, provide a good product, distinguish your product through branding, and develop a good sales system. If you get these elements aligned, you're headed for success. Again, demand of your product, company financials, and business operations all need to be in order as well for you to reap wholly the fruits of your labor.

BEING AWESOME THROUGH AUTHORITY MARKETING AND CONTENT MARKETING

One proven and measurable way to *up your game* and *highlight your awesomeness* is through authority marketing and content marketing. The awesome RP puts the Authority Marketing-

Content Marketing Connection to work consistently to elevate his or her game. Here are a few ways we help our client RPs shine as the awesome authorities they are.

GET VISIBILITY THROUGH PUBLIC SPEAKING

As an authority in your market, you have knowledge and experience to share. Public speaking puts you on the path to realizing your bold vision. We hope you didn't freeze up at the mere mention of public speaking. Many rate speaking in front of others as one of their top fears. Public speaking, though, can be a natural, comfortable, and fun way to brand you as an expert and up your game.

How do you get started in public speaking? Let's say that you have a well-attended women's show coming to your city and that traditionally you book a booth or table at the show. As a way to improve your presence, visibility, and authority level, you could reach out to the organizers of the show and ask to get a few moments on stage to share your professional expertise.

Be sure to frame the request in a way, however, that makes clear how the show attendees and show organizers will benefit from your "share" time on stage. You may get asked the same questions repeatedly by your customers and by being able to use the platform of public speaking to answer questions on everyone's mind, you've provided a great value to the audience, the value of your time.

Instead of spending money on advertising and TV commercials where you're pushing your message *out*, when you have something of value people want, when you have the information and knowledge they need, *they'll be drawn to you.* Creating marketing energy that draws people to you will entirely change your marketing approach. Consider public speaking as a way to market with authority.

BUILD CREDIBILITY BY PUBLISHING BLOGS, E-BOOKS, AND WHITEPAPERS

Another way to be awesome and up your game is to market your business with authority through the publication of e-books and whitepapers on your website. You may have blog content articles already. Blogging is an amazing way of marketing with authority. If, though, you can take that content, convert it into an e-book, and add visually stimulating graphic design that matches your brand, you can create something your target market can download from your website and save to their desktop. By offering e-books and whitepapers, the RP positions himself or herself as an authority.

Additionally, you can market your business with authority by publishing content on your website through your blog. Blog-writing businesses are commonplace now. You can hire a company or freelance writer to write on your behalf. The quality of some of these services, of course, is questionable. What you should look for when hiring a company to blog for you is that they understand the mind of your audience. What we've experienced is that website companies that write blog content are concerned mostly with writing content friendly to search engines. These companies may be plugging in the right keywords, but they're not creating content aptly positioned for target market or sticky content their fan base feels compelled to share.

Don't be fooled, future Rockstar Professional, *all content is not created equal.* The RP's content is valuable, interesting, relevant, and shareable. If you're going to hire a company to blog for you, hire a qualified authority marketing company such as RMI that specializes in authority and content marketing. You've made Level 1 gains by setting your bold vision; don't lose ground at Level 2 by skimping on highly valued content. Making the right moves at Level 2 positions you to amplify your business even greater in Level 3.

LEVEL 2 AMPLIFIERS AND TWEAKS

AMPLIFIERS

1. Visit the websites of three of your competitors and write down the tagline they use to communicate what makes them unique.
2. Write down what makes your business unique and compare it to what your competition is saying. Reflect on whether the messages are too similar. If so, set a goal to improve your business and marketing messaging.
3. Send out a survey to your recent customers asking them to share their thoughts on your business to gain insight into how they perceive you.

TWEAKS

1. If you cannot communicate easily to others what makes your business unique, spend time brainstorming ways to improve your customer's experience or the product you sell so that they are different from your competition.
2. If you've been operating with the same unique selling proposition for a period and find your new business interest leveling off, add some lagniappe to the mix.
3. If you find interest still waning, perform a SWOT analysis. Perhaps market conditions have changed, and you need to reevaluate and redefine your USP.

LEVEL 2 DIALERS AND DRAINERS

DIALERS

1. Compile a list of recent client testimonials and post them to your website. Read them frequently to reflect on the positive impact you're making on others.
2. Remind yourself of your story and celebrate your story with your fan base by hosting a brand birthday celebration. Invite your customers to celebrate with you.

3. Take a public speaking class or join an organization, such as Toast Masters International, that provides lots of public-speaking practice.
4. Set, achieve, and celebrate milestones in video content creation. It's your XX (whatever number) episode!

DRAINERS

1. Customer service issues can hurt your reputation and send customers running to your competition. Ensure systems and processes are in place for customers to communicate problems with you before it affects your business.
2. Don't forget your own story or try to be something you're not. It's important to stay relevant and grow with the times, but never forget your branded story. Forgetting your roots can drain marketing energy.

PLANNING TO ROCK

Smart Marketing Planning,
Strategic Marketing Decisions

We've dealt with several business truths as we've made gains on Level 1 and Level 2. Here's another truth: *Marketing takes time and money*. Yeah, you may be thinking, *everyone knows that*. Perhaps, but has everyone considered which has more value, time or money? Probably not. With some marketing decisions we've witnessed and their poor results, we feel safe in saying that not enough time is spent thinking about the value of time and money. Otherwise, businesses would make more marketing decisions that are smart and strategic.

So, which has more value, time or money? Well, the truth (yes, another truth) is that both have relative value, and choosing one over the other when it comes to strategic marketing would be ill advised. We propose that those striving to be Rockstar Professionals learn to make strategic marketing decisions based on committing a marketing budget, creating a solid marketing action plan (MAP) with SMART marketing goals, conserving time and money through amplified marketing, and choosing strategic tactics that "play" the "6 Strings of Marketing." These important factors make a star appearance in our Level 3 gains, which we refer to as the 4 Cs of Strategic Marketing.

THE LEVEL 3 GAINS: THE 4 Cs OF STRATEGIC MARKETING

- Committing to a Marketing Budget
- Creating a 1-page Marketing Action Plan (MAP)
- Conserving Your Time and Money
- Choosing Tactics Strategically

LEVEL 3 KEY TERMS

Marketing Action Plan. A 1-page document that outlines in 8 sections business specifics in regards to marketing: consumer problem, target audience, proposed solution, unique selling proposition, channels, revenue streams, cost structure, and key metrics.

Marketing Strategy. A specific marketing action, driven by a strong, functional marketing action plan (MAP), usually expressed with precise action verbs.

Marketing Tactic. A tool or system used to execute a marketing strategy.

LEVEL 3 SELF-ASSESSMENT

Answering the following yes/no questions to gauge your current Level 3 readiness achievement:

1. We know what stage our business is in and recognize that a plan is needed to move it to the next stage.
2. We will set aside time to create our 1-page marketing action plan.
3. We recognize that a marketing plan is important for ensuring our entire team is on the same page.
4. We make marketing decisions based on a strategic plan and budget.

If you answered yes to all four questions, way to go! Now, get ready to rock as we direct our energies into smart planning and strategic marketing. If you did not answer yes to each question, that's OK. We'll be sharing lots of valuable information, and you'll begin to realize the way in which time and money can work *with* you to plan smarter and make strategic marketing decisions. In addition, you'll leave Level 3 with greater clarity about how to conserve your time and money through amplified marketing. And, if that's not enough to excite you, you'll earn Level 3 gains by creating your 1-page marketing action plan. So, let's waste no time moving through Level 3 and get on our way to becoming the Rockstar Professionals we were meant to be!

COMMITTING TO A MARKETING BUDGET

Not many of us like to admit that we're limited on time and

RMI POV

Set your annual marketing budget before you make marketing decisions to save time and money. To measure results for improved future decision making, tie the amount spent to the results of each effort.

money. We all know it's true, but sometimes we like to believe we have more time than we do and more money for marketing than is realistic at our business stage and for our business type. We also make a fatal assumption when it comes to marketing: *We assume that today's buyer was yesterday's buyer and, furthermore, will be tomorrow's buyer.* This assumption is dangerous for marketing budgets that value both time and money. The Rockstar Professional realizes that today's consumers are on a new path to purchasing, sometimes referred to as "the new buyer's journey."[4]

TODAY'S BUYER'S JOURNEY

In a time when the corporate sales reps ruled, not so long ago really, the buyer's journey[5] could be charted by the acronym AIDA: Attention, Interest, Desire, Action. To understand better that buying path, let us briefly turn to Hollywood and a modern movie classic *Glengarry Glen Ross*.[6] Chronicling two days in the office life of property salesmen, the movie serves as a cynical glimpse into the mindset of the old buyer's journey. Actor Alec Baldwin, in the role of Blake (perhaps the most prickish of sales execs in modern movie history), is sent by company owners Mitch and Murry to rile up the frontline salesmen of Premier Properties, reps struggling to sell parcels of land with the crappiest of sales leads.

Baldwin's character stands before the beleaguered salesforce, played superbly by the veteran actors Jack Lemmon, Ed Harris, and Alan Arkin, and slams them for not being "closers." He spins a movable chalkboard, doubling as a sales board, around to reveal our buyer's journey, with our tired reps as journey guide. Attention. Interest. Desire. Action. It's a journey about guiding the buyer down a narrow path to purchase.

By contrast, today's buyer's journey is not rep-led, at least not to such a degree as in the past. In fact, more than half of the buyer's journey is completed before speaking with a rep.[7] The new buyer's journey is about awareness of a need, buyer research, and considering solutions. Only after much content absorption, the new buyer makes a decision. Today's buyer wants—needs even—*lots* of content in order to make their informed decision. The RP's role in this new journey is to provide content and be the authority that, in place of the tired sales rep, is connected and available with solutions to the new buyer's needs. Today's buyer's journey is in a way shorter and longer than before. This journey takes 3 steps: awareness, consideration, decision.[8] These can, however, be wide-reaching steps, which again demand plentiful content in order to reach a decision.

So, if the new buyer's journey is heavily dependent upon content and salespeople are not so involved in stoking the flames of purchasing action, what then is the modern business owner or marketer to do? Where is his or her place on the buyer's journey? Our suggestion is for a shift from the "sales" mindset to a collaborative "consultant" way of thinking—and marketing.

In this new way of thinking, though, time and money still matter. We come back to the realization that all businesses, no matter their size, have a limited amount of time and a limited amount of money—and now the added factor of marketing toward the new buyer's journey. Committing to a marketing budget that respects these factors means creating SMART marketing goals. These SMART goals, then, should lead to making strategic marketing decisions based on creating touchpoints on the new buyer's journey. At RMI, we help our clients define those touchpoints and create tactics that meet the buyer at those places in the buyer's journey.

The RP's marketing budget must be based on today's market and today's buyer. This fact is another great reason why we remind our clients that marketing demands consistent, careful reevaluation and refinement of strategies and tactics. It's not a one-shot deal. Our clients are constantly on the stage and receiving feedback from their audiences. They're engaged and interacting in the market and with their customers. Their marketing budgets reflect the fact that they are committed to keeping "top of mind." This commitment pays off in customer need awareness, engagement, and decision making.

Here are a few reminders about committing to a marketing budget based on today's buyer's journey:

- Today's buyer is becoming aware of needs. Needs that you can frame as a problem best solved by your product or service.

- Defining strategic touchpoints on the buyer's journey may take working with a highly qualified marketing team. The DIY approach may be insensitive to your time limitations.
- Inconsistent marketing efforts will cause the new buyer to disengage. The new buyer will look to others, often your competition, to fulfill needs and solve problems.
- Today's buyer wants a dialogue with you. Providing content starts—and continues—that conversation. Automating the dialogue saves you time.
- Today's SMART marketing budget must reflect the realities of your time and money, *and* it must be a commitment to today's buyer. This commitment can be expressed in your marketing action plan.

CREATING A 1-PAGE MARKETING ACTION PLAN

Keeping the new buyer's journey in mind, your marketing foundation and success ultimately depends on the strength of your planning. Strategic marketing comes down to creating a solid marketing action plan (MAP). Time and experience have taught us that if your MAP is not strong or functional, marketing on its own cannot sustain your marketing plan long term. The drafting of a solid MAP is one aspect of RMI's Action Marketing Platform™ proven approach. It's helped us rock our clients' images and businesses to advanced levels of renown and success.

RMI POV

Overly complicated marketing plans are a waste of time and money. By creating a 1-page MAP (Marketing Action Plan) you'll have a road map for marketing decisions that is useful and effective.

DETERMINE THE POINTS ON YOUR MAP

The following steps will guide you through the basics of developing your MAP. Even if you've been in business for some time, we advise taking the time to go through this exercise. A strong MAP is necessary for moving through Level 3 and can take you a long way toward becoming a Rockstar Professional:

1. **Define the problem.** To be successful in business, your product or service must serve a need or solve a problem. Remember today's buyer's journey. Why are you needed? What is the problem that your business solves?
2. **Define your target audience.** Once you've solved the problem, determine the ideal target audience for your product or service. Never say, "It's for everyone!" That's not defining a target audience. Whom specifically will you serve? Outline a profile of the ideal customer, including where they shop, live, and work, and what they care about. You may have multiple audiences, but if you do, they will need to be defined separately. Also, think through the

ultimate customer experience. Consider all of the various touchpoints you'll experience with a customer as they find and interact with you, purchase from you, and stay connected to your brand after the sale.

3. **Propose your solution.** Propose the solution in a short, succinct manner easily understood by others. Don't make it complicated or overly wordy.
4. **Outline your unique selling proposition (USP).** Almost every business has competition. Even the most original of ideas may have competition because consumers have choices for fulfilling a need or solving a problem. Your competition may be indirect, but you still have competition. It's vital you know and communicate what makes your product or service different so that the consumer can have a reason to choose yours over others.
5. **Define your channels.** The best way to define the channels in which you will communicate your marketing messages is to meet your customers on their ground. If your customers engage with certain social media channels, watch certain TV shows, visit specific parts of town or specific websites, you'll want to be found in those spots.
6. **Outline your revenue streams.** In general, a revenue stream is any way in which money comes into your business. You may have one or many. Define the various ways money comes in and which ways are most profitable.

7. **Develop your cost structure.** Your cost structure includes the various types of expenses you will incur when creating products or delivering a service. Some costs will be fixed and some will change over time (variable). The cost structure of the firm is the ratio of the fixed costs to variable costs.
8. **Define key metrics.** Key metrics may include the number of customers you have, the number of users, average sale amount, number of transactions per customer, length of memberships, customer level, sales targets, and expenses. Define whichever items are key to your success or failure in order to measure them.

Developing a marketing action plan doesn't need to be an overly complicated task or require an MBA. By outlining the key concepts of a business foundation, you will be well on your way to launching a business that has the potential for success. Furthermore, you may find as your business and SMART goals grow that your time/money realities place you in a good position to work with a qualified marketing team, such as RMI.

FOCUS ON YOUR UNIQUE SELLING PROPOSITION

In Level 2 we asked you to define your unique selling proposition (USP), your "claim to fame," that differentiated you from your competitors and showcased you as the better choice for your

DETERMINE THE POINTS ON YOUR MAP

PROBLEM	CHANNELS
TARGET AUDIENCE	REVENUE STREAMS
SOLUTION	COST STRUCTURE
USP	KEY METRICS

target consumer. In the previous section, we introduced the marketing action plan (MAP) and asked you to consider your USP as a critical point on your MAP. Let's examine, now, ways in which you can focus more on your USP and the marketing results that focus could generate.

We could have titled this section "So What?" because that's the question your potential customers are asking themselves. When it comes to awareness of their needs and awareness of your product or service to fulfill those needs, they're asking, *So what? And, today's buyer has many more questions of you.* Your USP and the content generated to highlight that unique selling proposition, is a set of continuous, consistent answers to their questions.

Along the way, today's buyer may find that you're not the right fit for their specific need, and that's OK. Specifically, that's OK because if you're not right for them, the fit will be wrong on both ends, which results in customer dissatisfaction and draining of your marketing energy. Know who your target customer is, build a connection to that customer, offer your USP, meet the customer at the right touchpoints, and let the customer make an informed decision.

Becoming a Rockstar Professional means, among many things, that *you* are the authority in your market. You're also an authority on your USP, communicating that proposition, and staying engaged with your customers, many of whom will become part of your avid fan base. Don't get sidetracked, or pushed offstage, by deviating from your unique selling proposition. At times, you'll step back to reevaluate and redefine, but that's still part of a concerted focus. The rock star who does not reevaluate and redefine unfortunately becomes irrelevant and "yesterday's sound." You need to be able to answer *So what?* before your customers ask.

MAKE SMART MARKETING GOALS

As an RP, you've defined your USP, you know the points on your MAP, and now you're ready to start making SMART marketing goals. SMART goals, or SMART criteria,[8] have been around for quite a while. The acronym is a mnemonic device for remembering a set of criteria around business objectives or goals. For our purposes, SMART stands for the following criteria: specific, measurable, achievable, results-oriented, and timely.

SPECIFIC: Focused on one thing to achieve

MEASURABLE: Tracked and measured through time

ACHIEVABLE: Realistic, not "pie in the sky"

RESULTS-ORIENTED: Contributes to business success

TIMELY: End date set

Setting SMART marketing goals unites a team, focuses the RP on results, and improves chances of success. Remember though, any goal cannot be a SMART goal by merely calling it so. True SMART marketing goals must be about achieving the right outcome for your business, given what you've learned about today's buyer. Consider the following not-so-SMART versus SMART marketing goals:

Example of a not-so-SMART goal: "I want to grow my business." This statement doesn't work as a goal because it's too vague and generalized. It's a wish or a dream, but it's not a goal. What makes a wish or a dream a *goal* is to make it SMART according to these goal-setting criteria. What makes it a SMART marketing goal is to tailor it to the new buyer's journey and today's marketplace.

Example of a SMART marketing goal: "I will book 3 public-speaking engagements by the end of the second quarter by networking through my service and business organizations to which my target customers belong." What makes this a SMART marketing goal is that it is specific, measurable, achievable, results-oriented, and timely.

At RMI, we remind our clients that setting goals, no matter how smart those goals, means little until taking *action*. Taking action is central to the proven approach of RMI's Action Marketing Platform.™ The next section offers an approach based on one's SMART marketing goals that lead into action by drafting and committing to a SMART marketing outline. Later, we will return to reexamine this action-oriented outline when we choose marketing tactics strategically by "playing" the "6 Strings of Marketing." What's important to focus on now is that you've reached a significant place at Level 3 where you're ready to draft your SMART marketing outline.

DRAFT A SMART MARKETING OUTLINE

Take a moment to applaud yourself for making SMART marketing goals. Celebrate the gains you're making at Level 3 of the AMP™ series. So far, at Level 3 you've committed to a marketing budget, created a 1-page marketing action plan (MAP), and made SMART marketing goals. Now you'll determine which area of your marketing system you need to improve. To do so, you'll draft an outline using your SMART marketing goals. After recording the focus area and goal, you'll ask why you're trying to achieve the goal, what actions you'll take to reach that goal, what amount of time the action requires, and specifically when the action will occur.

GOAL OUTLINE

A. Focus: The area of focus.
B. SMART goal: What you are trying to achieve.
C. Why: Why you are trying to achieve it.
D. Actions: The actions you'll take to reach your goal.
E. Time to complete: The amount of time it takes to complete the marketing effort.
F. Scheduled time: Specific time you'll take action on the goal.

EXAMPLE GOAL 1

A. Focus: Visibility.
B. SMART goal: Improve quality website viewers by 10 percent from 1,000 views a month to 1,100 views per month.

C. Why: Increasing the amount of quality website visitors to my website will increase my chance for cross promotion.

D. Actions:

   a. Blog twice a month.
   b. Add social share buttons.
   c. Cross promote with colleague.

E. Time to complete: 4 hours per month.

F. Scheduled time: Tuesday evenings from 4:00 to 8:00 p.m.

EXAMPLE GOAL 2

A. Focus: Conversions.

B. SMART goal: Improve quality online lead conversions from 10 per month to 12 per month.

C. Why: Increasing lead conversions on my website will result in 2 extra sales.

D. Actions:

   a. Review all website copy and USP.
   b. Ensure each page has clear call to actions.
   c. Add a lead capture generator to the home page of the website.

E. Time to complete: 6 hours plus $75 professional services.

F. Scheduled time: 3rd week of the month.

As you review drafting a SMART marketing outline and consider appropriate action steps for your SMART marketing goals, remember that key to the 4Cs of Strategic Marketing is the concept of *conservation*. From the onset of your RP marketing efforts, be thoughtful about your time and money expenditures. Your marketing energy will be drained if you are physically, emotionally, spiritually, and financially drained. Your SMART marketing outline respects your time and money.

Try setting your own SMART marketing goals.
Complete the outline for each goal.

GOAL 1

A. Focus:

____

B. SMART goal:

____

C. Why:

____

D. Actions:

 a. ______________________________

 b. ______________________________

 c. ______________________________

E. Time to complete:

____

F. Scheduled time:

____

GOAL 2

A. Focus:

____

B. SMART goal:

____

C. Why:

____

D. Actions:

a. ______________________________

b. ______________________________

c. ______________________________

E. Time to complete:

____

F. Scheduled time:

____

GOAL 3

A. Focus:

____

B. SMART goal:

____

C. Why:

____

D. Actions:

a. ______________________________

b. ______________________________

c. ______________________________

E. Time to complete:

____

F. Scheduled time:

____

Need assistance creating your
MARKETING ACTION PLAN?

Learn more about Rock My Image's consulting services at
RockMyImage.com/amplify

SMART Goals are Smart Business

Business owners face a myriad of challenges in running a business that not only include marketing challenges, but also operational, human resource, and financial issues, and more. While facing those challenges, it is important to have systems in place for setting goals, tracking progress, and measuring results. Business coaches integrate SMART Goals into every client's business planning process.

Business owners can benefit from a business coach in the same way a professional athlete benefits from having a coach: for motivation, development, and results. Business coaches and consultants use SMART goals as a way of getting team members moving together in the same direction and for integration into a strategic plan.

Visit www.rockmyimage.com to learn more about our business coaching and marketing consulting services.

CONSERVING YOUR TIME AND MONEY

Benjamin Franklin said, "Lost time is never found again." Why, you might ask, are we quoting a "Founding Father" of the United States in a book about marketing? It's simple: Benjamin Franklin rocked! When it came to life in the 1700s, in early America and in Europe, Franklin was an RP.

One reason, we believe, Franklin rocked in all his business dealings and his public life was that he understood the value of time. Another reason is that he understood the true nature of money, what it could do for us . . . and *to* us. Likely, we've all heard Franklin's famous "A penny saved is a penny earned," but have you heard some of his other sayings regarding money? Of the compelling power of money, Franklin stated, "He that is of the opinion money will do everything may well be suspected of doing everything for money."[9] The RP rooted in his or her core values will likely take such wisdom to heart.

We imagine our RP Ben would agree with us that conserving our time is like giving ourselves extra money. A good way to think about conserving your time is that your marketing time should be proportionate to your business type and stage and aligned with your SMART marketing goals.

For example, let's consider two business professionals: Andrea A. and Brian B. Both professionals are running their own businesses. Their basic business profiles look like this:

- **Andrea A.'s business profile:** Established high-end clothing boutique, B2C, retail, sole proprietor, location, not time critical, single purchase, quality focus.

- **Brian B.'s business profile:** Startup commercial real estate agency, B2B, service, LLC, extended entry, single purchase/rent, quality focus.

Now that we know more about their basic business profile, let's consider their current marketing decisions and behaviors.

- **Andrea A.'s marketing:** Andrea spends lots of time meeting with media reps and online posting on social media. She likes "creating dialogues" about the market and her store. She sees marketing as a social opportunity and doesn't see the need to measure the results of her efforts as her store generates consistent revenue, though profits have not increased in the past several years. She spends a lot advertising in local magazines and television spots each month, especially as she's grown close to the media reps who visit her, sometimes at the expense of paying off company and personal debt. She often complains of feeling "wiped out," and her employees feel she doesn't pay enough attention to day-to-day operations.
- **Brian B.'s marketing:** Brian loves working on his startup commercial real estate business. He created his own website and business cards, which took considerable time but cost very little. He's made a few sales through connections within his circle of family and friends. He's hoping his new website will bring clients in. By his own admission he's "not much of a talker" and doesn't enjoy networking, but he loves studying the commercial markets. He ran an ad in a few local papers and got a few phone calls from those spots. Though he does not

RMI POV

At certain points in your business, time may be more valuable than money and vice versa. For maximum results, be diligent about when to spend time and when to spend money.

currently engage in social media, he is considering creating a social media page on a popular website for the exposure.

Both Andrea and Brian have had some experience with marketing their businesses, and, remarkably, both feel they've had very positive experiences and results. Given our understanding of them and our discussions on committing a marketing budget and creating a 1-page marketing action plan, which one is doing a better job, *a strategic job*, of marketing? Which one is on the way to becoming a Rockstar Professional?

The answer is clear: neither.

It's unfortunate, but true, that neither Andrea nor Brian have learned and put into practice the lessons of committing a marketing budget or creating a solid MAP. Neither have taken time to create SMART marketing goals or draft a SMART marketing outline. Both have been marketing, but not like an RP markets—smart and strategic.

Why are both failing at amplifying their businesses? Or, asked a different way, what should both being doing when it comes to marketing their businesses like a Rockstar Professional? Andrea and Brian should be amplifying their businesses by committing a marketing budget, recording the points on their specific marketing action plan, and setting SMART marketing goals as part of a marketing plan based on action, such as the proven approach of RMI's Action Marketing Platform.™

Sadly, Andrea's and Brian's business profiles mean very little to them. If they're going to rock their businesses, they have to rethink what they understand about certain aspects of marketing:

- Themselves
- Their unique selling propositions
- Their marketing action plans
- Their SMART goals
- Their SMART marketing outlines

You'll notice that the description of their marketing decisions and behaviors mentioned little to nothing about these aspects of marketing.

In contrast, let's consider Chris C., also growing his own business, but like a Rockstar Professional. Chris is in a growth-stage medical practice. In addition, he has several business partners and a mixed quality/quantity focus. Chris has learned to conserve his time and to maximize his marketing dollar by collaborating with a qualified marketing agency such as RMI.

What makes the difference for Chris is that through committing a marketing budget, creating a functional marketing action plan, setting SMART marketing goals, and drafting a SMART marketing outline, Chris will make strategic marketing decisions that lead to *executing the right marketing tactics at the right time*. Unlike Andrea, Chris's business won't stay flat for years, and unlike Brian, Chris won't shy away from marketing and grow too little. Chris has learned and practiced a way of thinking and acting that amplifies, boosts, and rocks his business.

CONSERVE TIME AND MONEY THROUGH AMPLIFIED MARKETING

At Level 3, the emerging RP is ready to consider the awesome power of amplified marketing. RMI's Action Marketing Platform™ proven approach draws from the power of amplified marketing. This method of marketing generates the energy needed to fuel today's buyer. Amplified marketing is dynamic, high-engagement, authority-centered marketing that "pulls" customers to you by providing expert knowledge and valuable information. Amplified marketing presents the RP as the expert. Furthermore, the RP—you—become the collaborator of need-fulfillment your customer seeks. This marketing energy is different from advertising that "pushes" your agenda on the buyer. By earning attention for your business through being an authority in your industry, you'll gain credibility and visibility.

Understanding fully the power of amplified marketing means understanding its varied marketing tools such as needs-driven digital content, authority-based publications, and public engagements. Also, it's understanding these tools in relation to how they funnel into an automated, documented marketing system. And, it's about bringing all the tools and systems together to build a consistent, authentic brand and brand story. At RMI, we rock amplified marketing for our clients. Remember that, ultimately, amplified marketing respects your time and money, largely because it leads into our final C of strategic marketing, choosing tactics strategically.

RMI POV

How you approach customers ranges from pushing or promoting sales on them to pulling or winning them over by establishing loyalty. RMI is a big proponent of pulling customers in by providing valuable content and sharing expertise.

CHOOSING TACTICS STRATEGICALLY

When we're planning smart and making strategic marketing decisions, we choose marketing tactics that have the best chance at producing outstanding results—the sort of results that make marketing worth our time and money. At RMI, we've proven that today's buyer responds best to amplified marketing.

Before we go further, it's worth noting the difference between a marketing strategy and a marketing tactic. Your marketing action plan, detailed earlier, helps you think through and problem solve for strategic marketing; it gives you clarity about where you are and where you're going. Your MAP points you in the correct direction toward your *marketing strategy*, the types of marketing actions you'll take based on the SMART goals stemming from your MAP (e.g., increasing social media presence, expanding content on your website, interacting with online influencers, etc.). You outline these strategies in your SMART marketing outline.

Marketing tactics are, however, the particular tools and systems you'll put into place with your strategy and with any accompanying logistics (e.g., adding a particular social networking site to your media presence and creating focused content for that site, or contacting a specific list of 5 influencers in your market for a MAP-driven survey). A marketing tactic becomes part of your marketing strategy; it is *not* the strategy itself. A strategy must have other components outlined, including specific times for application and overall time estimates for completion.

When you commit a budget and make a strong marketing action plan, and then you use that MAP to set your SMART goals and inform your marketing strategies and tactics, you'll be using your time and money wisely and experiencing better marketing results with less stress and headaches. All your effects will be directed and thoughtful, based on solid facts, evidence, and data. You'll feel less drained, emotionally and financially, and, most important, you'll be creating lots of positive marketing energy through your amplified marketing.

PLAY THE 6 STRINGS OF MARKETING

The 6 Strings of Marketing helps our clients identify weak and strong points in their marketing efforts. It's part of how we help our clients conserve their time and money, and we believe it can help you, too, as you become a Rockstar Professional. In addition, playing the 6 Strings can help you imagine and visualize tactics that may put your SMART marketing goals into action.

Depending on your current place in the amplified marketing process, you may need to adjust your focus on different "strings" at different times. The 6 strings are visibility, lead generation, conversions, average number of sales per customer, average dollar sale per transaction, and profit margin:

6 STRINGS OF MARKETING

- **Visibility:** Be found by the right customers in the right places.
- **Lead Generation:** Create new business inquiries.
- **Conversions:** Improve the quality of a lead to get the right type of customer.
- **Average Number Sales/Customer:** Increase the number of times a customer buys.
- **Average Dollar Sale:** Increase the dollar per sale amount.
- **Profit Margin:** Decrease expenses, improve efficiencies, and automate where possible to improve the bottom line.

CHOOSE ANCR TACTICS AS TOUCHPOINTS

If the days of AIDA are gone, or at least waning, what tactics guide today's buyer toward your product or service? We explored earlier that the new buyer's journey is about awareness, consideration, and decision. Providing content to establish yourself as an authority will position you in the "consultant" role today's buyer seeks. Still, you may be left asking, *What tactics do I use?* As we've stated before, AMP™ is not a one-size-fits-all approach. It's not "marketing in a bottle." Which tactics are best should be based on your committed budget, MAP, SMART marketing goals, and strategies drafted in your SMART marketing outline. What we can tell you is that you can think about the tactics as ANCR. We can definitely proclaim this marketing message: *Good-bye AIDA, Hello ANCR!*

ANCR is a way to remember a process that runs tandem to the buyer's journey and "touches" the buyer at strategic points:

- A—acquire tactics
- N—nurture tactics
- C—convert tactics
- R—retain tactics

In *Boost Your Business: The Rockstar Professional's Guide to Marketing Success, Volume 2* we explore more in-depth particular tactics used to acquire, nurture, convert, and retain customers through amplified marketing. The important lesson for Level 3 is to commit a marketing budget, create a solid 1-page marketing action plan, set SMART marketing goals, and draft a SMART marketing outline.

Also important at this level is to conserve your time and money through marketing strategies and tactics that focus on amplified marketing. *Let your strategic marketing tactics pull rather than push customers to you.* Playing the 6 Strings of Marketing can help you create specific tactics to meet your SMART marketing goals while respecting your time. All this is meant to keep you centered and focused while on the marketing stage and to generate lots of positive marketing energy for amplified results.

A Systems Success Story

As a private practice physician with ambitions to grow into a regional name, Dr. James St George knows the importance of maximizing every dollar in his marketing budget. After decades of building a successful practice, an improved approach was needed to take his business to new heights and achieve his goal of multiple practice locations in less than 2 years.

St Johns Vein Center is an example of using the ANCR (Acquire, Nurture, Convert, Retain) approach to not only generate leads but nurture each lead, convert them to a sale, and retain the patient for additional services as well. All in just 2 years. An example of this in action is how visitors to his website are invited to engage in vein health assessments and to receive automated emails with helpful video content and articles and monthly newsletters with relevant, shareable, and interesting content. SJVC has achieved double-digit growth in every metric, and Dr. St George has expanded his practice to multiple locations.

Visit stjohnsvein.com

LEVEL 3 AMPLIFIERS AND TWEAKS

AMPLIFIERS

1. Create a 1-page marketing action plan (MAP).
2. Reflect to see if your MAP and SMART marketing goals align with the updated marketing budget.
3. Draft a SMART marketing outline for each SMART marketing goal with specific amplified marketing tactics.
4. Use the 6 Strings of Marketing to "play though" your current marketing tactics and make movements toward amplified marketing.

TWEAKS

1. Create a spreadsheet with last year's marketing expenditures broken down into categories (e.g., print ads, online ads, printing, etc.). Create ways to measure the effectiveness of each expenditure category.
2. Using last year's budget, make projections and tweaks for the current year based on the results or outcome of the individual expenditures.

LEVEL 3 DIALERS AND DRAINERS

DIALERS

1. Connect with likeminded business owners in your community to share experiences, resources, and ideas. Having others to reach out to you is a great way to fuel your mind and business.
2. Listen to business thought leaders you admire who show evidence of consistently evaluating their marketing plans and setting SMART goals for themselves.
3. Celebrate achievement of your SMART marketing goals. Share those achievements with your fan base in content that gives them the credit they deserve for helping you achieve those goals. Don't forget to thank your customers.

DRAINERS

1. Once you have clear goals, a marketing action plan, and a budget, making marketing decisions becomes exponentially easier. You'll be empowered to decline sales calls respectfully with reps or companies selling new advertising opportunities that don't align with your goals.

2. Remember the A in SMART. Nothing is more draining than setting goals that are not realistically achievable. Once you've set and achieved a SMART goal, you'll be inspired to reach a bit higher with the next goal. Be inspired by your own bold vision!

SUMMATION
LEVEL 1-3 GAINS AND MOVING FORWARD

The business owner or professional who rocks his or her business—like the rock star who makes it to the main stage and stays there—finds that focusing on his or her purpose, passion, and gifts generates energy that leads to smart, strategic marketing. Whether it's initial, emerging, or amplified authority and content marketing, your strategies and tactics will be successful when informed by a strong, functional marketing action plan.

Each of the 3 Levels presented in this book are part of a larger plan, what we call our Action Marketing Platform™ series. We hope this book has provided insight, structure, and inspiration on your journey in business. Our goal was to create a book that would introduce you to the 11 Levels of our Marketing Action Platform™ and lay the foundation for a successful amplified marketing effort. In the process, we hope we've provided knowledge that will save you time and money.

The intended results of this book were that you gain ground on the following levels:

1. Get in tune with your clear objective, bold vision, inspired mission, and reasoned motivation;
2. Sharpen your awareness of your business and your unique selling proposition; and
3. Plan to rock with smart marketing planning and strategic marketing decisions.

The next books in the AMP™ series, *Boost Your Business: The Rockstar Professional's Guide to Marketing Success Volume 2* and *Rock Your Business: The Rockstar Professional's Guide to Marketing Success Volume 3*, will focus on Levels 4-7 and Levels 8-11 respectively. Please continue reading after this summation for a sneak peek at volume 2.

If you've found this book helpful, please pass it on to a business owner or marketing manager you believe it may benefit. We understand that some business owners and marketing managers may be looking for one-size-fits-all and magic-trick approaches to marketing, and we're glad our approach is neither of these. What the AMP™ proven approach aims to do is provide a responsible, systematic, and relevant means to growing your business—and with amazing results.

We hope you'll continue to seek your purpose, ignite your passion, and share your gifts with others through your business and marketing. Please visit RockMyImage.com/amplify for accompanying blog posts, articles, videos, assessments, downloads, and more.

SOUND BITES

A PREVIEW OF LEVELS 4-7

Boost Your Business: The Rockstar Professional's Guide to Marketing Success Volume 2

If you found volume 1 of the AMP series, *Amplify Your Business*, motivating and informative, we know you'll learn even more and be boosted to higher levels of marketing achievement with volume 2, *Boost Your Business.*

In volume 2, we explore Levels 4-7 of the 11 Levels of AMP™.

Level 4: Moving Onto the Marketing Stage—The 3 Pillars of Marketing

Level 5: Positioning Yourself as an Authority for Maximum Results—Your Look, Culture, and Reality

Level 6: Turning Customers into "Fans"—The Right Tools for the Job

Level 7: Maximizing Your Marketing Investment—Understanding Profitability

Highlights of volume 2 include marketing strategies and tactics that will boost your business. Imagine the marketing heights you could reach by extending your knowledge base and marketing practice to include the following:

- The 3 Pillars of Marketing: branding, tools development, and marketing
- Becoming the authority in your industry
- Applying the ANCR principle (Acquire, Nurture, Convert, Retain) for sales leads
- Strengthening your sales funnel
- Understanding the buyer's journey by identifying touchpoints and common conversations
- Learning how to calculate profitability for your unique business
- How to avoid the trap, and the cost, of "No Action"

We hope you'll join us as we move through Levels 4-7 on our way to becoming Rockstar Professionals. Your inner Rockstar is waiting!

NOTES

LEVEL 1

1. Tracking down a reliable reference for this statistical claim proved an intriguing exercise. Eric T. Wagner used this statistic, cited from Bloomberg.com, in his piece "Five Reasons 8 out of 10 Businesses Fail" for Forbes.com, September 12, 2013, http://www.forbes.com/sites/ericwagner/2013/09/12/five-reasons-8-out-of-10-businesses-fail/#3cd4f5665e3c. The original source for this alarming statistic may have come from Karne E. Klein's article for Bloomberg.com in 2002, in which Klein stated a finding by the National Restaurant Association that 80% of independently owned restaurants fail within the first two years: "The Bottom Line on Startup Failures," Bloomberg.com, March 4, 2002, http://www.bloomberg.com/news/articles/2002-03-03/the-bottom-line-on-startup-failures. Klein also reports figures from the US Commerce Department that roughly 20% of new businesses survive after five years. A good document to learn more on the subject is the SBA's "Frequently Asked Questions about Small Business," September 2012, https://www.sba.gov/sites/default/files/FAQ_Sept_2012.pdf. Regardless of the actual number of new businesses that fail in the first two years, the Rockstar Professional will make every conceivable attempt not to fail, including amplifying, boosting, and rocking their businesses through the AMP™ proven approach.

LEVEL 2

2. "The Science of Storytelling: Why Telling a Story is the Most Powerful Way to Activate Our Brains," Leo Widrich, *Lifehacker* [blog], December 5, 2012, http://lifehacker.com/5965703/the-science-of-storytelling-why-telling-a-story-is-the-most-powerful-way-to-activate-our-brains.

3. "Neocortex," *Wikipedia*, last modified March 14, 2014, https://en.wikipedia.org/wiki/Neocortex.

LEVEL 3

4. "Part 1 – What Is the New Buyer's Journey?" Jason Robinson, MarketBridge, March 12, 2014, http://www.market-bridge.com/2014/03/12/ultimate-guide-new-buyers-journey-part-1/.

5. "The Modern Buyer's Journey: How to Sell in 2016," Leslie Ye, *Hubspot* [blog], December 15, 2015, http://blog.hubspot.com/sales/the-new-buyers-journey.

6. "*Glengarry Glen Ross*," *Wikipedia*, last modified March 23, 2016, https://en.wikipedia.org/wiki/Glengarry_Glen_Ross_(film).

7. This statistic is accredited online to the B-2-B research and advisory group SiriusDecisions (www.SiriusDecisions.com). We found it quoted in "Understanding the Buyer's Journey," Pardot, accessed February 22, 2016, http://www.pardot.com/buyer-journey/.

8. "The Modern Buyer's Journey: How to Sell in 2016," Leslie Ye, Hubspot [blog], December 15, 2015, http://blog.hubspot.com/sales/the-new-buyers-journey.

9. "Top 5 Famous Benjamin Franklin Quotes on Money – Personal Finance Wisdom & Lessons," Pat S., Money Crashers, accessed February 24, 2016, http://www.moneycrashers.com/famous-ben-franklin-quotes-money-finance/.

LINER NOTES

Behind every successful small business owner stands an army of people willing to provide advice, resources, and encouragement. Sometimes we wish these people could just hand us checks instead (which would ease the way incredibly), but since rich friends are hard to find, we would like to thank the following individuals and companies for their support of our agency:

Sarah Harper - for your support and loyalty

Olaf Guerrero - for your creative talents

Our Clients - for inspiring us to create and grow

Kimberly Smith Ashley - for taking our book idea and making it a reality and better than we could have dreamed kmsmithwrites.com

Summer Morris - for bringing our book to life with awesome design skills sumodesignstudio.com

There are too many people to name that have supported the Rock My Image team on our journey, and we thank each of you for your referrals, social media shout outs, friendship, advice, insights and talents. You rock!

JEN DeVORE RICHTER

The entrepreneurial journey is not one I could embark on alone. Without the loving support of my husband, Will, I would have had to go get a corporate job years ago! His unfailingly positive attitude and encouragement, even when I felt like giving up, has been immensely appreciated and does not go unnoticed. Thank you, Will, for being a man of God and for your love and understanding in helping me reach my goals.

To Mitch and Cate, I'm really proud to be a part of your lives and can't wait to see what the future has in store for you. I love you both!

I also dedicate this book to my Dad, Dave DeVore, who always made me feel capable and loved. I am so grateful to have had such an awesome dad. I love you, Paca!

Thank you to my awesome family for loving me: my brother Jeff, his wife, Julie, and their three children: Caylie, Cooper, and Chloe; my brother James and his wife, Jenny, and my goddaughter Alexia.

Ultimately, all of the creative gifts we have come from God. I am humbled daily by the unending love He shows me. I am proud to be His daughter and give all praise to the Lord Jesus Christ.

KENNY HARPER

I want to thank all the guiding stars in my life, the people who helped me overcome any strife.

Thanks to my wife, Kathy, for being a true soulmate & my boys Kenny and Michael for fueling my will to create.

Thanks to my family for believing in me and giving their unconditional love & to the friends that inspired me and helped me rise above.

Thanks to the people who took time to show me a better way & those who truly listened to what I had to say.

Thanks to those who inspired me to create a bold vision & those who contributed to me achieving my mission.

Thanks to the challenges in my life that helped me to grow & realize a reality that I once didn't know.

I have thanks and gratitude for all my blessings & I'll keep moving forward and keep on pressing.

Dedicated to be a guiding star like the ones who have guided me, a life long commitment that I guarantee.

Thank you ALL for being yourself and being true! *Live Life & Love*; that's what we're here to do.

MANNY TORRES

My better half is a phrase that is often thrown around without regard to its true meaning. In my case, my wife, Mary Beth, is truly my better half and the foundation my world is based on. Mary Beth provides inspiration through her passion and tenacity to achieve her goals and to have her voice heard. She is always by my side, ready to make me laugh or lend me a hand when needed. Thank you, MB, for your unwavering love and support.

I also dedicate this book to my family, including my parents, who raised me to be courteous and industrious, and always to command my own destiny. Love you, Mom and Dad!

Thank you to my brothers, Todd and Mark, who by tormenting me taught me how to be resilient and determined. They also showed me that competition brings out the best in all of us. Although you are both older, you always treated me as your contemporary, which made me work extra hard to be on your level. I'm proud to be your little brother.

There are countless others who have helped me over the years, far too many to include here. Whether through swimming, water polo, networking, design, marketing, or having a beer, you all have contributed to making this possible, and I thank you!

THE READER

To YOU, the reader, THANK YOU for your support and your business. We hope this book inspires and empowers you to become a ROCKSTAR PROFESSIONAL!